MISDEFEND these hands WITH ME
WITH ME
Mark Horton

D1247675

MASTER POINT PRESS • TORONTO

Master Point Press
214 Merton St. Suite 205
Toronto, Ontario, Canada
M4S 1A6   (647) 956-4933

Email:	info@masterpointpress.com
Websites:	www.masterpointpress.com
	www.teachbridge.com
	www.bridgeblogging.com
	www.ebooksbridge.com

Library and Archives Canada Cataloguing in Publication

Title: Misdefend these hands with me / Mark Horton.
Names: Horton, Mark (Mark Howard), author.
Identifiers: Canadiana (print) 20210190779 | Canadiana (ebook) 20210190825
| ISBN 9781771400633
   (softcover) | ISBN 9781771405720 (PDF) | ISBN 9781771407182 (HTML)
| ISBN 9781771407687 (Kindle)
Subjects: LCSH: Contract bridge—Defensive play.
Classification: LCC GV1282.42 .H67 2021 | DDC 795.41/53—dc23

Editor	Ray Lee
Copy editor/Interior format	Sally Sparrow
Cover design	Olena S. Sullivan/New Mediatrix

1 2 3 4 5 6 7   24 23 22 21

Acknowledgments

I am indebted to Andrew Robson's column in *The Times,* Brian Senior's column in *The Daily Telegraph*, Sally Brock's column in *The Sunday Times, IBPA Bulletin* Editor John Carruthers and Wolf Klewe. All have been invaluable in bringing suitable deals to my attention. Ron Tacchi was the guinea pig who attempted to solve the problems to ensure that they were neither too easy nor too difficult, rather, as Goldilocks would say, 'Just right'.

Table of Contents

INTRODUCTION

Play Bridge with Reese, published in 1960, introduced the now popular method of presenting a deal using an 'over the shoulder' style. The follow up in 1976, *Play These Hands with Me,* was even more successful. In 2007 my attempt to follow in the footsteps of the master, *Misplay these Hands with Me,* describes how a series of hands are plausibly misplayed before the eponymous author realizes there was a better, winning line. It did not prove difficult to gather material from top-class events. The book spawned a series of articles that ran in the ACBL Bulletin from 2011-2020.

Although there will never be a shortage of misplayed hands, it occurred to me that it was time to approach the concept from a different angle, and I discovered that my files were awash with deals from major championships where one (or sometimes both) of the defenders had failed in their mission. On many occasions the winning defense was found at another table, a testament to the tremendous standard set by today's experts.

Defense is difficult. Just like declarer play, it requires the ability to attempt to reconstruct the hidden hands, in this case, declarer's and partner's. This process starts during the bidding phase and continues with the opening lead, which is often a vital moment. After the appearance of dummy it is usually possible to form some sort of overall defensive plan, but the devil may prove to be in the details. In the unlikely event that you miss the winning move on a deal, I should remind you that Reese was fond of using the phrase, 'I should have got that right'.

I invite you to *Misdefend These Hands with Me.*

Mark Horton
Shrewsbury

The Hasty Heart

There can be little doubt that team events represent the 'purest' form of the game. With overtricks reduced to a minor role, both declarer and the defenders can concentrate on making or breaking the contract.

In the qualifying rounds of a long knockout event where my partner is a sound performer, I pick up this average collection as South:

> Dealer West.   ♠ A Q 6 2
> Both Vul.   ♡ A 7 3
>   ◊ J 10
>   ♣ 10 8 6 3

The player on my left opens 1♠ and when partner has nothing to say, East responds 2NT, which is alerted. Upon inquiry this proves to be a somewhat unusual agreement, promising a limited hand (8-12) with both minor suits. I have nothing to contribute and West rebids 4♠, leaving us with this brief auction:

West	North	East	South
1♠	pass	2NT*	pass
4♠	all pass		

My partner leads a fourth-best ♡5 and dummy is as promised:

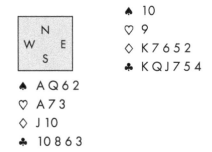

    ♠ 10
    ♡ 9
    ◇ K 7 6 5 2
    ♣ K Q J 7 5 4

♠ A Q 6 2
♡ A 7 3
◇ J 10
♣ 10 8 6 3

That does not look too terrifying — I have two trump tricks and as partner's lead promises an honor in hearts we may be able to defeat this, as they say, 'on the go'.

I take the ♡A, declarer following with the ♡10, cash the ♠A to remove dummy's trump, and continue with the ♡7. Declarer wins with the king (partner following with the ♡2) and plays the ♠K, followed by the ♠J. I win with the queen as partner discards the ♣9 and the ♡4. Evidently partner has the ♣A, but when I return the ♣3 declarer ruffs, draws my remaining trump with the ♠9 and proceeds to play out his remaining trumps.

This is the position:

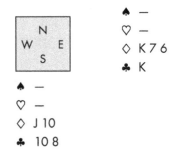

    ♠ —
    ♡ —
    ◇ K 7 6
    ♣ K

♠ —
♡ —
◇ J 10
♣ 10 8

When declarer produces the ♡Q it squeezes my partner in the minors.

This was the full deal:

```
                  ♠ 8
                  ♡ J 8 6 5 4 2
                  ◇ Q 4 3
                  ♣ A 9 2
♠ K J 9 7 5 4 3                      ♠ 10
♡ K Q 10            ┌───────┐        ♡ 9
◇ A 9 8            │  N    │        ◇ K 7 6 5 2
♣ —                │ W   E │        ♣ K Q J 7 5 4
                   │   S   │
                   └───────┘
                  ♠ A Q 6 2
                  ♡ A 7 3
                  ◇ J 10
                  ♣ 10 8 6 3
```

POST-MORTEM

In general terms, leading away from a king is a losing proposition, so there was no guarantee that North would hold the ♡K.

In the other room, my counterpart found a much more effective defense. Having taken the ♡A, he returned the ♠2. Declarer won with dummy's ten and advanced the ♣K, ruffing when South played an unconcerned ♣3. The ♠K was taken by the ace and now South found the way to avoid all danger by switching to the ◇J. When he came in with the ♠Q he could continue with the ◇10, breaking up the impending squeeze.

There are two lessons to be learned from this deal. Firstly, the importance of retaining trump control — the ace of trumps frequently has an important role to play. Secondly, one must try to anticipate how the play will develop — here it is clear that North will need to hold useful cards in both diamonds and clubs.

In a knockout match, my partner is of the highest caliber, while our opponents consistently win a large number of masterpoints. Towards the middle of the last set, with the issue still in doubt, I pick up these cards sitting South:

> Dealer South. ♠ A K J 9
> N-S Vul. ♡ K Q 7 5 3
> ◇ 6
> ♣ Q J 6

I open a Precision 1♣, promising at least 16 points, and when West overcalls 1♡ my partner doubles, which shows roughly 5-8 points. When East has nothing to say, I have to consider three possibilities: I could pass, playing for a penalty, bid 1♠ (despite the lack of a fifth card in the suit) or resort to an unorthodox 1NT. Unable to decide between the first two, I fall back on the third and rebid 1NT. West now jumps to 3◇ and when East raises to 4◇, he goes on to 5◇. My partner doubles this, but West is not finished and comes again with a redouble, concluding this dramatic auction:

West	North	East	South
			1♣*
1♡	dbl*	pass	1NT
3◇	pass	4◇	pass
5◇	dbl	pass	pass
redbl	all pass		

My partner leads the ♡2 and dummy does not appear to be threatening:

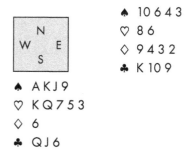

                    ♠ 10 6 4 3
                    ♡ 8 6
                    ◇ 9 4 3 2
                    ♣ K 10 9

            ♠ A K J 9
            ♡ K Q 7 5 3
            ◇ 6
            ♣ Q J 6

Declarer plays dummy's six, takes my queen with the ace and then plays the ◇A, followed by the queen. Partner wins with the king and, in response to my encouraging signal in spades, returns the ♠2. When I play the king declarer ruffs, cashes the ◇J and then plays the ♡4 to dummy's eight. I try ducking, but declarer plays a club to the ace and pitches a club on the ♡J. I can win that, but declarer then shows his cards.

 This was the layout:

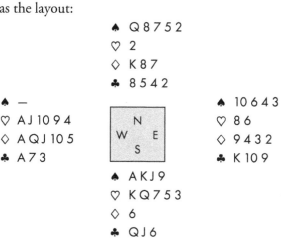

                    ♠ Q 8 7 5 2
                    ♡ 2
                    ◇ K 8 7
                    ♣ 8 5 4 2

    ♠ —   ♠ 10 6 4 3
    ♡ A J 10 9 4   ♡ 8 6
    ◇ A Q J 10 5   ◇ 9 4 3 2
    ♣ A 7 3   ♣ K 10 9

                    ♠ A K J 9
                    ♡ K Q 7 5 3
                    ◇ 6
                    ♣ Q J 6

Not for the first time, Trick 1 is all-important. South must cover dummy's ♡6 with the seven! Declarer wins and will continue with the ace and queen of diamonds, but North wins and exits with a diamond to dummy's nine, South discarding a couple of spades. Declarer plays a heart to the queen and ace and can then throw a club on a heart, but the ♡53 will be good for a trick and declarer must go one down.

In the other room West overcalled South's 1♡ with 2◇, and when East jumped to 4◇ he went on to 6◇, doubled by North, who led his heart. South did not find the play of covering the ♡6 with the ♡7 and declarer won and returned the ♡4. If North had ruffed this the contract would have been two down, but when he discarded declarer took eleven tricks. We lost 14 IMPs, but a dreadful misplay a few deals later saw us gain 18 back and survive.

TEN PIN

The board-a-match teams format is perhaps the most challenging form of duplicate, as the slightest slip can result in the loss of a board. All the players know the moves when I find myself looking at this hand as South:

Dealer South.	♠ 10 9 5 4 3
E-W Vul.	♡ Q 2
	◇ K 10 6 4
	♣ K 6

When I pass, West does the same, but my partner opens 3♣. When East passes, I briefly consider bidding 3NT as a tactical maneuver, but as a passed hand that has significantly less value and I elect to pass. Now West comes to life with 3♡ and East responds 4♣, obviously showing a good hand. That gives me the opportunity to make a conventional double, which in our methods promises a high honor in clubs, the idea being to help partner with the lead. West's 4♡ leaves us with this auction:

West	North	East	South
			pass
pass	3♣	pass	pass
3♡	pass	4♣	dbl*
4♡	all pass		

My partner leads the ◇5, revealing this dummy:

```
              ♠ A K 8
    ┌─────┐   ♡ A K 7
    │  N  │   ◇ Q J 8 2
    │W   E│   ♣ 7 3 2
    │  S  │
    └─────┘
  ♠ 10 9 5 4 3
  ♡ Q 2
  ◇ K 10 6 4
  ♣ K 6
```

East had an awkward bid over 3♣, but once West balanced, it was clear to go to game. When declarer calls for dummy's ◇Q, I cover with the king. Declarer wins with the ace and plays two rounds of trumps, partner following with the eight and nine, and continues with dummy's ♣2.

If declarer has the ♣A, playing low will leave me exposed to a possible endplay at some point, so I put up the ♣K. Declarer follows with the nine and partner overtakes with the ♣A, cashes the ♣Q and then plays the ◇3. Declarer goes up with dummy's jack and proceeds to cash four rounds of hearts. This is the position when the last of them is played:

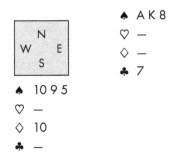

♠ A K 8
♡ —
◇ —
♣ 7

♠ 10 9 5
♡ —
◇ 10
♣ —

When partner discards the ♠2, declarer throws dummy's club, and in order to hold on to the master diamond I also have to part with a spade. That means dummy's spades are good and declarer records a vital overtrick.

This was the layout:

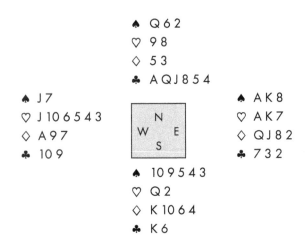

♠ Q 6 2
♡ 9 8
◇ 5 3
♣ A Q J 8 5 4

♠ J 7
♡ J 10 6 5 4 3
◇ A 9 7
♣ 10 9

♠ A K 8
♡ A K 7
◇ Q J 8 2
♣ 7 3 2

♠ 10 9 5 4 3
♡ Q 2
◇ K 10 6 4
♣ K 6

This was the position when declarer played his last trump:

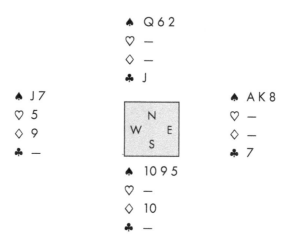

North had to hold on to the ♣J so was forced to throw a spade. Having done its work, the ♣7 went from dummy and I was also forced to part with a spade.

It would not have helped if my partner had played a third round of clubs, as in the ending I would still have to throw a spade, allowing declarer to play the ♠J, killing my ♠109.

The winning defense is to retain the ♣K earlier. North can win the first round of clubs and play a second diamond, setting up a trick for my ten while I still have an entry in clubs.

No defender found the line of ducking the club, but it is clear to do so. If West has something like:

♠ J 7   ♡ J 10 6 5 4 3   ◇ A 9 7   ♣ A 10

then after declarer has ruffed a spade, South could be endplayed on the second round of clubs. However, in that scenario North might well have led a top club, knowing that South held the ace or king.

Had partner led a low club at Trick 1, the advantage of our convention would have been clear — three rounds of clubs enable South to score a trick with the ♡Q.

We lost the board.

My partner in the qualifying round of a major Pairs event is a decent player, prone to the odd flight of fancy and a predilection for playing for singleton kings offside — particularly in the club suit. My South hand is distinctly average:

> Dealer West.   ♠ J 10 7 6
> Both Vul.   ♡ A J 6 4
> ◇ 5 3
> ♣ A 6 3

When the player on my left opens with a weak 2♠, my partner has nothing to say and East responds with a forcing 2NT. When West rebids 3◇ to show a near-maximum in high cards, East jumps to game, leaving us with this simple sequence:

West	North	East	South
2♠	pass	2NT*	pass
3◇*	pass	4♠	all pass

My partner leads the ♣Q:

```
                       ♠ A K
          ┌───────┐    ♡ 8 7 5 2
          │   N   │    ◇ A Q J 7 6
          │ W   E │    ♣ 8 2
          │   S   │
          └───────┘
          ♠ J 10 7 6
          ♡ A J 6 4
          ◇ 5 3
          ♣ A 6 3
```

It looks as if my hand is going to be worth three tricks, so we will need to find one more. Partner's lead could be from the ♣KQ or ♣QJ — the king would ask for count in our methods, the queen for attitude. As partner is likely to be leading from length I am inclined to place him with the ♣QJ, so I put up the ♣A. When declarer follows with the ♣5,

I switch to the ♡A. We play attitude signals on the ace and queen, and when declarer follows with the ♡10, partner contributes an encouraging ♡9. Without giving the matter much thought I continue with the ♡4, but declarer ruffs, unblocks dummy's spades, returns to hand with a diamond and plays two more rounds of trumps, claiming the rest after I have taken my ♠J.

This was the full deal:

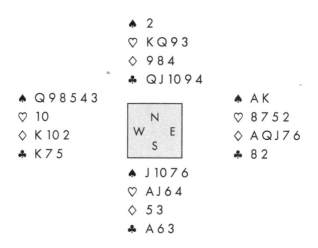

```
                    ♠ 2
                    ♡ K Q 9 3
                    ◇ 9 8 4
                    ♣ Q J 10 9 4
    ♠ Q 9 8 5 4 3          ♠ A K
    ♡ 10          N        ♡ 8 7 5 2
    ◇ K 10 2    W   E      ◇ A Q J 7 6
    ♣ K 7 5       S        ♣ 8 2
                    ♠ J 10 7 6
                    ♡ A J 6 4
                    ◇ 5 3
                    ♣ A 6 3
```

POST-MORTEM

My defense would have been correct if declarer were, say, 6=2=2=3. In that scenario, if I switch back to clubs at Trick 3, declarer wins with the ♣K and plays on diamonds. I can ruff the third round, but declarer overruffs, goes back to dummy with a trump and plays another diamond, leaving me helpless. On the actual layout, the club switch is correct. I will be able to ruff the third round of diamonds and lead another club.

Things might have been easier if partner had started by leading a top heart. If he elects to begin with the king, I can give count with the six, after which a club switch should make it clear that we only have one trick in hearts, thereby simplifying the defense.

Events for mixed partnerships have always been popular; at one time there were events in England which awarded a 'flitch' prize to the leading married couple, recalling the annual tradition in some English villages of presenting a 'flitch', or side of bacon, to a couple who did not regret their marriage.

Playing in the European Mixed Teams against a famous married partnership, I pick up this modest collection as South:

> Dealer North.   ♠ K J 6 5
> Both Vul.   ♡ J 6 5
>   ♢ 10 9
>   ♣ Q 9 8 3

When my partner passes, the player on my right opens 1NT, promising 12-14, and that is raised to game, leaving us with this simple auction:

West	North	East	South
	pass	1NT	pass
3NT	all pass		

As West has made no attempt to find a major-suit fit, I decide to start with the ♠5 and dummy is revealed:

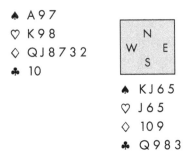

> ♠ A 9 7
> ♡ K 9 8
> ♢ Q J 8 7 3 2
> ♣ 10
>
>   ♠ K J 6 5
>   ♡ J 6 5
>   ♢ 10 9
>   ♣ Q 9 8 3

Declarer plays dummy's seven and partner produces the ♠Q. She returns the three to my jack, declarer following with the two and ten and again withholding dummy's ace. When I play the ♠K, declarer wins and plays a diamond to the king and a second diamond. Partner takes the ace and cashes a spade, but declarer then claims the rest.

This was the full deal:

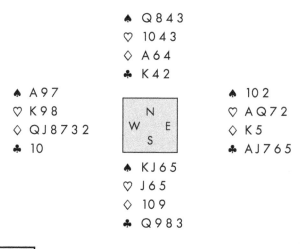

```
                    ♠ Q 8 4 3
                    ♡ 10 4 3
                    ◇ A 6 4
                    ♣ K 4 2
   ♠ A 9 7                          ♠ 10 2
   ♡ K 9 8          N               ♡ A Q 7 2
   ◇ Q J 8 7 3 2  W   E             ◇ K 5
   ♣ 10              S              ♣ A J 7 6 5
                    ♠ K J 6 5
                    ♡ J 6 5
                    ◇ 10 9
                    ♣ Q 9 8 3
```

POST-MORTEM

After Trick 2, I knew that the spades were 4-4. If declarer held the ◇AK and the ♣AK there would be nine tricks, but that was clearly impossible, as declarer would hardly duck in spades, risking a perspicacious switch from, say, ♡J65, finding partner with ♡AQ10x. That indicates partner must have at least one high club and/or a high diamond. If partner has the ◇A and the ♡A then I can safely continue with a third spade, but if anyone has two aces it is more likely to be declarer. If she has the ♡A, ◇K and ♣A then it is clear that playing a third spade will be too slow and the only hope for the defense is for me to switch to a club at Trick 3.

From a practical point of view, it was also possible for partner to work this out at Trick 2, but returning a spade is the type of play that it is easy to make without thinking.

In the other room, West was the declarer and North led a fourth-best ♠3. That should have pointed declarer to the winning line but she ducked twice and was lucky to survive when North played a third spade.

In this event, 22 pairs reached 3NT, and the contract was never defeated.

We are nearing the end of the European Mixed Teams Championship when I pick up these cards as South:

Dealer West.   ♠ A 8 4
Both Vul.   ♡ Q 8 7 6 5
                ♦ 5 4 3
                ♣ 10 5

When the dealer passes, my partner opens 1♡, which promises a limited hand with at least four hearts. East overcalls 2♦ and, with a nod to Larry Cohen, I raise to 3♡. West comes to life with a double, and when my partner passes, East bids 4♣. When West continues with 4♠ everyone passes, leaving us with this auction:

West	North	East	South
pass	1♡	2♦	3♡
dbl	pass	4♣	pass
4♠	all pass		

Partner leads the ♡9 (third and fifth) and dummy is displayed:

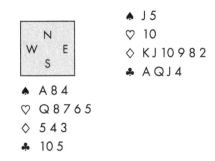

                        ♠ J 5
                        ♡ 10
                        ♦ K J 10 9 8 2
                        ♣ A Q J 4

        ♠ A 8 4
        ♡ Q 8 7 6 5
        ♦ 5 4 3
        ♣ 10 5

I play the queen and declarer wins with the ace and plays the ♦6. My partner takes the ace and switches to the ♣3. When declarer plays dummy's four, I put up the ten and declarer wins with the king, ruffs a heart, pitches a heart on the ♦K and plays the ♠J. That runs to partner's king and she exits with a club. Declarer wins with the jack, ruffs a diamond and plays the ♠9. I win with the ace and play a heart, but declarer ruffs and plays the ♠Q, claiming when we both follow. This was the layout:

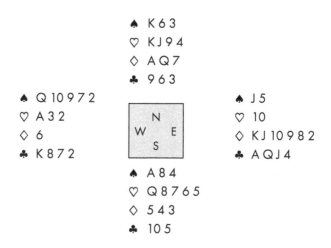

                    ♠ K 6 3
                    ♡ K J 9 4
                    ◇ A Q 7
                    ♣ 9 6 3

    ♠ Q 10 9 7 2   ♠ J 5
    ♡ A 3 2   ♡ 10
    ◇ 6   ◇ K J 10 9 8 2
    ♣ K 8 7 2   ♣ A Q J 4

                    ♠ A 8 4
                    ♡ Q 8 7 6 5
                    ◇ 5 4 3
                    ♣ 10 5

POST-MORTEM

There were several ways to defeat this contract (a trump lead for example, when after two rounds North has an easy heart switch), but after the early play, it was asking a lot for partner to switch to a spade after taking the ◇A. The club switch was fine, but I should have risen with the ♠A and played a second club. That way I will score a club ruff. I should have got that right, but partner might have given me a wake-up call by following to the second round of hearts with the king rather than the four. This would be a clear indication that she held something useful in spades.

Playing in a brand-new Mixed Teams event that offers an opportunity to advance to the World Championships, I pick up this modest collection as South:

Dealer North.   ♠ Q J
Neither Vul.   ♡ Q 10 8 7 6
                     ◇ A 7 3
                     ♣ 9 7 3

After two passes, I decide to chance my arm by opening 1♡. West overcalls 1NT and East, doubtless looking for a spade fit, responds with Stayman, jumping to 3NT when West denies holding a four-card major. This is the complete auction:

West	North	East	South
	pass	pass	1♡
1NT	pass	2♣	pass
2◇	pass	3NT	all pass

Ignoring my opening bid, my partner leads the ◇10:

                               ♠ A 9 8 6
                               ♡ J 5 4 3
                               ◇ 8 6 4
                               ♣ K J

        ♠ Q J
        ♡ Q 10 8 7 6
        ◇ A 7 3
        ♣ 9 7 3

I take the ace, declarer following with the two, and return the seven, covered by the jack and queen. Partner exits with the ◇9 and declarer wins with the king and plays the ♣2 to the four, jack and my three. When declarer continues with dummy's ♡3, I play the seven and am somewhat disconcerted to see declarer insert the nine, which holds the trick, partner playing the two. When declarer now plays the ♣5, partner takes the ace, cashes the ◇5 and exits with the ♠3. Declarer wins with the king, and then cashes the ♡AK and the ♣Q before playing a spade to dummy's ace. Partner follows with the ten, which means the ♠9 is declarer's game-going trick.

This was the full deal:

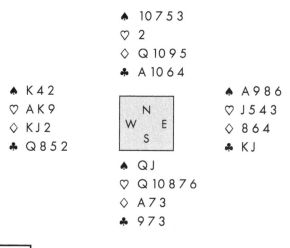

This was the position when declarer cashed his last heart:

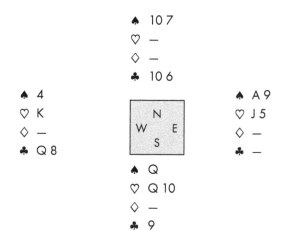

North was squeezed in the black suits. I could have prevented this by playing the ♡10 on the first round of the suit. Declarer can score three heart tricks, but only by using up a vital entry to dummy.

In the other room, North led the ◊5 and the defenders played three rounds of diamonds, declarer winning and playing a club to the jack. When it held she played a second club. North won, cashed the ◊10 and exited with the ♡2, making it easy for South to put in the ♡10. Declarer could cross to dummy with a spade to take the heart finesse, but there was no squeeze so we lost 10 IMPs.

Only four of thirty pairs made 3NT.

No Excuse

8

Playing in a one-day Swiss Teams event, my partner is a brilliant, but at times mercurial, player while our other pair comprise our sponsor and her somewhat irascible partner. Against unknown opponents I hold as South:

Dealer North.   ♠ J
E-W Vul.   ♡ Q 4 3
               ◇ Q 5 4
               ♣ K Q J 10 8 6

When my partner opens 1♡, East overcalls 4♠. Given the vulnerability, that must show quite a good hand, so I decide to compete by introducing my suit. Over my 5♣ West raises to 5♠, and partner's double concludes this lively auction.

West	North	East	South
	1♡	4♠	5♣
5♠	dbl	all pass	

I lead the ♣K and dummy appears to be of little value:

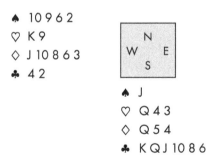

♠ 10 9 6 2
♡ K 9
◇ J 10 8 6 3
♣ 4 2

♠ J
♡ Q 4 3
◇ Q 5 4
♣ K Q J 10 8 6

The first trick is completed by the two, five and three. My king asked partner to give count, so I can be reasonably sure he has three clubs including the ace — with two he would almost certainly have overtaken and returned the ♣5. Mindful of partner's opening bid I switch to the

♡3, promising an honor. However, declarer wins in hand with the jack, draws trumps and claims eleven tricks.

This was the layout:

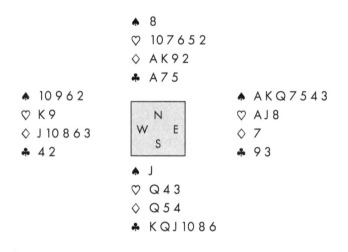

Partner was not slow to apologize — he could have overtaken the ♣K and cashed the ◊K. The appearance of my ◊4 would then make it clear to go back to clubs.

From my point of view it would have been better to continue with the ♣Q (or possibly the ♣J), relying on partner to do the right thing. If partner does not have the ♡A then overtaking should be clear-cut.

In the other room, 5♣ was passed out and West saw little point in leading a spade. Declarer won the lead of the ◊J in dummy, drew trumps, played a diamond to the queen, a diamond to the nine and pitched a spade on the ◊A. After ruffing a spade, declarer exited with a heart and the defenders could not untangle their tricks.

LOST CONTACT

9

The 1980s were a golden age for bridge congresses in the United Kingdom, but now they are mostly a distant memory, although there are still some enjoyable events in Scotland and Ireland. The promise of the odd pint of Guinness has lured me to the Emerald Isle, and towards the end of the Congress Pairs we have every chance of winning when I pick up these cards as South:

Dealer West.	♠ 8 7 4 3
N-S Vul.	♡ A J 2
	◇ A 9 5 4
	♣ A 5

West and my partner have nothing to say and East opens 1◇. Our opponents are playing Precision, so the bid says nothing about the diamond suit and promises a maximum of 15 points. I daresay some players would double with my hand, but I have never seen the merit of doing that with a balanced hand and I elect to pass. West responds 1NT and, when that gets back to me, I decide that as the opponents appear to be limited it is reasonable to compete. I double, which ends the auction:

West	North	East	South
pass	pass	1◇*	pass
1NT	pass	pass	dbl
all pass			

If East's bid had promised real diamonds, my delayed double would have suggested that I had a powerful holding in the suit, but in this instance, I have only shown a desire to compete. My partner leads the ♠10 and dummy is nothing to write home about:

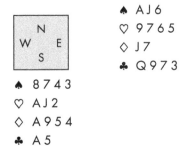

♠ A J 6
♡ 9 7 6 5
◇ J 7
♣ Q 9 7 3

♠ 8 7 4 3
♡ A J 2
◇ A 9 5 4
♣ A 5

There is no accounting for taste; it would not occur to me to open with these cards, whatever the system. Partner's conversion of my double suggests we have the balance of power, so I am hopeful we can defeat the contract.

Declarer plays low from dummy; when I follow with the ♠7 he wins with the queen and plays the ♣10, on which partner contributes the four. I win with the ace and have to decide how to continue. Declarer should not have a four-card major and it looks as if partner has three or four clubs. I am inclined to place declarer with length in diamonds, so I decide to stay passive and return the ♠3 to the five, two and jack. Declarer continues with a club to the jack, and when that holds he plays the ♣6, partner winning with the king as I discard the ◇5. Partner continues with the ♠9 to dummy's ace, declarer discarding the ◇2.

When declarer cashes dummy's ♣Q, I discard my remaining spade and declarer discards the ◇6. A low heart to the queen holds, declarer exits with a diamond and my partner wins with the king and cashes the ♠K. I am down to ♡AJ ◇A9 and one way or another declarer is sure to take one more trick so we are -180.

This was the full deal:

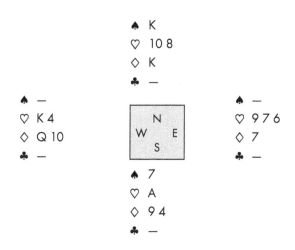

	♠ K 10 9 2	
	♡ 10 8 3	
	◇ K 3	
	♣ K 8 4 2	
♠ Q 5		♠ A J 6
♡ K Q 4	N	♡ 9 7 6 5
◇ Q 10 8 6 2	W E	◇ J 7
♣ J 10 6	S	♣ Q 9 7 3
	♠ 8 7 4 3	
	♡ A J 2	
	◇ A 9 5 4	
	♣ A 5	

POST-MORTEM

Partner's opening lead was unlucky. However, if we go back to the point where declarer cashed the ♣Q, I should have parted with the ♡2, rather than my last spade. Suppose declarer now plays a heart. There are several ways in which the defenders can prevail.

If I play the ♡J, declarer wins and will probably exit with a diamond. (If declarer ducks a heart to my now bare ace the last round of spades squeezes him in the red suits.)

If partner plays low on the diamond, I win with the ace and play my remaining spade in this position:

	♠ K	
	♡ 10 8	
	◇ K	
	♣ —	
♠ —		♠ —
♡ K 4	N	♡ 9 7 6
◇ Q 10	W E	◇ 7
♣ —	S	♣ —
	♠ 7	
	♡ A	
	◇ 9 4	
	♣ —	

Declarer is caught in a very rare position — a criss-cross squeeze by the defenders! If he throws a heart, North wins and plays a heart, taking the last two tricks with the ◇K and the ♡10. A diamond discard allows North to cash the ◇K and then exit with a heart, giving South the last two tricks.

As for declarer's play, having won a club trick he could have abandoned the suit and turned his attention to diamonds, playing low towards the jack. Suppose I win with the ace and return a spade. Declarer wins in dummy and plays a heart to the queen, followed by the ◇Q. North wins and can cash the black queens, but the second of these squeezes South (down to ♡AJ ◇95) and declarer takes two more tricks.

I make a note to send the deal to David Bird.

It's All in the Mind

Playing in a Mixed Team trials with a top-class partner, I pick up a promising collection as South:

Dealer South.	♠ Q 7 3
N-S Vul.	♡ A
	◇ Q 7
	♣ A K Q J 9 7 2

When I open 1♣, West overcalls 1♠ and his partner raises to 3♠, suggesting a limited hand with four-card support. When I bid 4♣, West continues with 4♠, which ends proceedings:

West	North	East	South
			1♣
1♠	pass	3♠	4♣
4♠	all pass		

My partner leads the ♣8 and dummy is not bad:

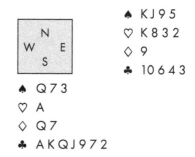

	♠ K J 9 5
	♡ K 8 3 2
	◇ 9
	♣ 10 6 4 3
♠ Q 7 3	
♡ A	
◇ Q 7	
♣ A K Q J 9 7 2	

When I play the ♣K, declarer ruffs, cashes the ◇AK pitching a club (partner following with the four and six) and ruffs a diamond with the ♠J. I overruff and play another club; declarer ruffs, ruffs a diamond with the ♠9 and plays the ♡2. After winning with the ace, I play a third club but declarer ruffs and plays two rounds of trumps, the last of these squeezing partner in the red suits for an overtrick.

This was the layout:

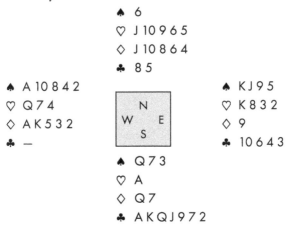

```
                          ♠ 6
                          ♡ J 10 9 6 5
                          ◇ J 10 8 6 4
                          ♣ 8 5
        ♠ A 10 8 4 2                      ♠ K J 9 5
        ♡ Q 7 4          ┌─────────┐      ♡ K 8 3 2
        ◇ A K 5 3 2      │    N    │      ◇ 9
        ♣ —              │ W     E │      ♣ 10 6 4 3
                         │    S    │
                         └─────────┘
                          ♠ Q 7 3
                          ♡ A
                          ◇ Q 7
                          ♣ A K Q J 9 7 2
```

POST-MORTEM

As long as declarer is careful, you cannot hope to defeat 4♠. However, it is vital to make life as difficult as possible and to that end you should smoothly discard a club on the third round of diamonds. If declarer now plays a heart, you win and play a club. If declarer ruffs and unsuspectingly plays a spade to the nine, you win with the queen and play another club. If declarer makes the mistake of ruffing this (discarding a diamond is required), it is no longer possible to take ten tricks.

In the other room, East-West bid all the way to 6♠, which South was happy to double. Declarer ruffed the club lead, cashed the ◇A, ruffed a diamond and played the ♡2 to South's ace. After ruffing the club return, declarer ruffed a diamond with the ♠K and ran the ♠J. When it held, declarer drew trumps via the marked finesse, the last of these squeezing North in the red suits.

A Switch in Time

The advent of the Internet has meant that bridge can be presented online in a variety of ways. During an individual event using board-a-match scoring, I am dealt these cards as South:

Dealer West. ♠ A K
Neither Vul. ♡ 10 7 3
◇ 10 5 2
♣ J 9 7 6 4

After West opens 1NT (15-17), East uses Stayman and, upon discovering that there is no major-suit fit available, settles for 3NT, leaving us with this brief exchange:

West	North	East	South
1NT	pass	2♣	pass
2◇	pass	3NT	all pass

My partner leads a fourth-best ♠6, which may have hit dummy's weak spot:

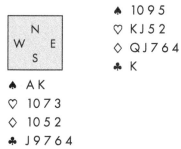

♠ 10 9 5
♡ K J 5 2
◇ Q J 7 6 4
♣ K

♠ A K
♡ 10 7 3
◇ 10 5 2
♣ J 9 7 6 4

To make it clear that I have only two spades, I win with the ♠A and then cash the king. Declarer follows with the two and jack while partner plays the ♠4. It seems that partner has the ♠Q so I will need to try to find an entry to his hand. If partner held the ♡A he would surely have played a higher spade on the second round, so it must be right to try one of the minors. Reflecting that if declarer needs a diamond finesse partner will always get in, I switch to the ♣6. This guards against the possibility that declarer has the ◇AK and the ♡AQ, but not the ♣A.

Declarer wins with dummy's king, partner following with the eight, comes to hand with a heart to the queen, and cashes the ♣AQ. Partner follows with the ten but then, having followed to the heart with the four, discards the ♡6. Declarer cashes the ♡A and then plays a third heart, cashing dummy's ♡KJ. My partner discards the ♠3 followed by the ♠8 to leave these cards:

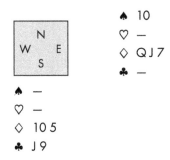

```
                               ♠ 10
                               ♡ —
                  N            ◇ Q J 7
              W       E        ♣ —
                  S
   ♠ —
   ♡ —
   ◇ 10 5
   ♣ J 9
```

After some thought, declarer exits with the ♠10. My partner, down to ♠Q7 ◇K9, can take two spades, but then has to lead into the split diamond tenace.

The full deal:

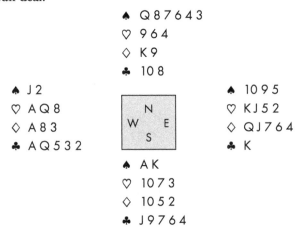

```
                      ♠ Q 8 7 6 4 3
                      ♡ 9 6 4
                      ◇ K 9
                      ♣ 10 8
   ♠ J 2                                ♠ 10 9 5
   ♡ A Q 8               N              ♡ K J 5 2
   ◇ A 8 3          W       E           ◇ Q J 7 6 4
   ♣ A Q 5 3 2          S              ♣ K
                      ♠ A K
                      ♡ 10 7 3
                      ◇ 10 5 2
                      ♣ J 9 7 6 4
```

South knew that the club suit was not threatening, so if the ♡A was missing declarer could not take more than eight tricks. Unless declarer was falsecarding, the ♠4 was not partner's lowest spade, so it was unlikely declarer was missing the ♣A. That points towards switching to a diamond, which would have ensured the defeat of the contract. Partner might have considered playing the ♠7 on the second round of the suit (with a suit headed by the ♠Q10, the ♠Q would be an easy way to indicate possession of the ♡A), but as it happens we did not lose the board! In the four-card ending at the other table, North elected to keep three spades and the ◇K and declarer read the position, playing a diamond to the ace to record a vital overtrick.

My partner in a board-a-match event is a thoughtful player with plenty of experience. We are making steady progress when I pick up this modest hand as South:

Dealer South.	♠ 10 9 7 4
N-S Vul.	♡ J 5 3
	◇ J 2
	♣ K Q 9 3

My left-hand opponent opens 1♠ and partner overcalls 2♠, which promises at least 5-5 in hearts and one of the minor suits. When East doubles, suggesting some interest in taking a penalty, I have nothing to say, and West's jump to 4♠ leaves us with this auction:

West	North	East	South
1♠	2♠ *	dbl	pass
4♠	all pass		

My partner leads a fourth-best ♡7 to reveal this modest dummy:

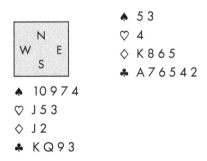

	♠ 5 3
	♡ 4
	◇ K 8 6 5
	♣ A 7 6 5 4 2

♠ 10 9 7 4
♡ J 5 3
◇ J 2
♣ K Q 9 3

When I play the jack, declarer wins with the ace and plays the ◇9. My partner takes that with the ace and after some consideration exits with the ♠K. Declarer wins with the ace, ruffs a heart, cashes the ♣A, ruffs a club and plays three rounds of spades. In with the ♠10, I force declarer with a club, but after ruffing, he cashes his last trump and catches my partner in a red-suit squeeze for what proves to be a vital overtrick.

The layout:

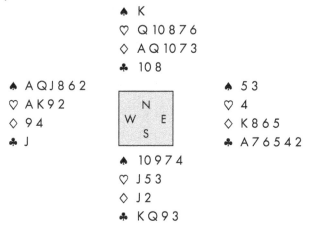

```
                      ♠ K
                      ♡ Q 10 8 7 6
                      ◇ A Q 10 7 3
                      ♣ 10 8
  ♠ A Q J 8 6 2                          ♠ 5 3
  ♡ A K 9 2            N                  ♡ 4
  ◇ 9 4            W       E              ◇ K 8 6 5
  ♣ J                  S                  ♣ A 7 6 5 4 2
                      ♠ 10 9 7 4
                      ♡ J 5 3
                      ◇ J 2
                      ♣ K Q 9 3
```

POST-MORTEM

One of the elements that it is essential to master in order to become a fearsome defender is being able to work out the distribution. On this deal it was not too difficult to determine that partner's shape was 1=5=5=2. Once you have done that, it should be possible to work out that partner will come under pressure in the ending unless the link to dummy is broken.

At the other table after a similar start, my counterpart, having taken a spade trick, returned a diamond, severing the link to dummy, thereby restricting declarer to ten tricks.

The Camrose Trophy, contested annually by England, Ireland, Scotland and Wales, is the world's oldest-running international bridge event, having begun in 1937. Although it has lost some of its glamour, it is still keenly fought. During one of the recent matches, I pick up a promising collection as South:

Dealer South.	♠ A 6
N-S Vul.	♡ A Q 10 9 8 7 4
	◇ A 2
	♣ 10 6

I open 1♡ and when West overcalls 2♣, my partner raises to 2♡. East now enters from the wings with 3♠, which upon enquiry proves to be natural and weak. Mindful of Meckstroth's Law[1], I rebid 4♡, but West continues with 4♠. I don't see us taking eleven tricks, and with no certainty of more than three in defense, I make a disciplined pass, leaving this sequence:

West	North	East	South
			1♡
2♣	2♡	3♠ *	4♡
4♠	all pass		

I start with the ♡A and see this dummy:

♠ 5 4
♡ J 2
◇ K Q 9 6
♣ A K 8 4 3

	N	
W		E
	S	

♠ A 6
♡ A Q 10 9 8 7 4
◇ A 2
♣ 10 6

---

1   When partner freely raises your six-card major, bid game.

I would not have overcalled with the West hand; the clubs are lacking both a sixth card and good intermediates, and it is not clear that a club will be the best lead should East-West end up defending.

My partner follows with the ♡3, and when declarer contributes the six I continue with a second heart. Declarer ruffs my partner's king, then plays the ♣2 to dummy's ace and the ♠4. When my partner plays the ♠8, declarer plays the nine and I win with the ace. I cash the ◇A and exit with a diamond, but declarer wins in hand with the jack, cashes the ♠KQ, collecting my partner's ♠J10, and claims.

The full deal was:

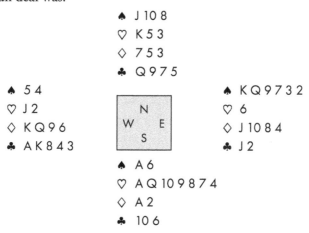

```
                    ♠ J 10 8
                    ♡ K 5 3
                    ◇ 7 5 3
                    ♣ Q 9 7 5
    ♠ 5 4                              ♠ K Q 9 7 3 2
    ♡ J 2              N               ♡ 6
    ◇ K Q 9 6      W       E           ◇ J 10 8 4
    ♣ A K 8 4 3        S               ♣ J 2
                    ♠ A 6
                    ♡ A Q 10 9 8 7 4
                    ◇ A 2
                    ♣ 10 6
```

POST-MORTEM

The opening lead is frequently a critical moment for the defense. It was a certainty that there would be no more than one heart trick. Given that the ♠A guaranteed South a quick entry, it would have been a better idea to start with the other red ace. Then it will be clear to continue with the ◇2. When South regains the lead with the ♠A, a low heart allows North to win with the king and return a diamond for South to ruff.

In the other room, South was able to start with an old-fashioned Acol 2♡. That kept West quiet and when North jumped to 4♡, East was unwilling to venture 4♠. Naturally, West started with a top club, but that gave up a vital tempo and after drawing trumps declarer could lead towards the ♣Q, establishing a discard for one of his losers.

The impact of the Coronavirus on bridge players was significant. With rubber bridge out of the question as a means of supplementing one's income, coaching sessions on Funbridge and BBO became an attractive option. During an IMP tournament where my partner is inexperienced but eager to learn, I am dealt these cards as South:

Dealer East.	♠ A J 7 3
Neither Vul.	♡ K J 8 5
	◊ K J 7 4
	♣ 5

When the player on my right opens 1♣, I double. West redoubles and after my partner passes East rebids 2♣, suggesting a hand with a long suit that is not interested in playing for penalties. West's jump to 3NT concludes the auction:

West	North	East	South
		1♣	dbl
redbl	pass	2♣	pass
3NT	all pass		

My partner leads a fourth-best ♠2.

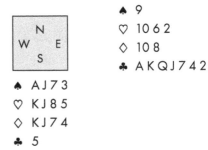

			♠ 9
			♡ 10 6 2
			◊ 10 8
			♣ A K Q J 7 4 2

♠ A J 7 3
♡ K J 8 5
◊ K J 7 4
♣ 5

I win with the ace, declarer following with the five. With seven club tricks in view, it is clear that if the contract is to be defeated I will need partner to hold one of the red aces. If partner's spades are headed by the ♠K10 then returning the ♠J should work, although even then, the location of the ♠8 will be important. Before I play a spade, I must also consider partner's possible holdings in the suit. As the ♠2 promises an honor, a suit headed by the ♠K10 or ♠Q10 is a possibility, but so is one containing only the ten.

On balance, it feels better to play a red suit, so I switch to the ◊J, catering for declarer holding say ◊Q62. Alas, declarer takes the ◊A, cashes the ♠KQ and then points to dummy's clubs.

This was the full deal:

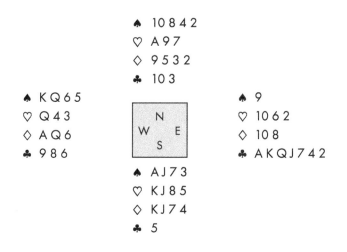

```
              ♠ 10 8 4 2
              ♡ A 9 7
              ◊ 9 5 3 2
              ♣ 10 3
♠ K Q 6 5                      ♠ 9
♡ Q 4 3          N             ♡ 10 6 2
◊ A Q 6       W     E          ◊ 10 8
♣ 9 8 6          S             ♣ A K Q J 7 4 2
              ♠ A J 7 3
              ♡ K J 8 5
              ◊ K J 7 4
              ♣ 5
```

POST-MORTEM

The decision to switch to a red suit was well-reasoned, but the devil was in the details. A red jack is correct, but if declarer has four diamonds the ◊J will not work, as partner's ◊A93 will not be good enough — he needs a fourth diamond. Switching to the ♡J only requires partner to hold three cards in the suit, headed by the ♡A9.

In the other room, East opened 3NT and my hand made the traditional lead of the ♠A. When dummy appeared, it was clear to switch to the ♡J.

It is always a pleasure to take part in a friendly International match, especially one that is played away from home. During a match against the Netherlands, I pick up this miserable collection as South:

Dealer East.	♠ K 7
N-S Vul.	♡ 3
	◊ J 9 6 2
	♣ 10 9 8 7 5 2

East opens 1♡ and is immediately raised to game over my pass. I am toying with the idea of making the 'movie-star' lead of the ♠K when I realize that the bidding is not yet over — my partner has overcalled 5◊ and when East advances to 5♡, he doubles, leaving us with this dramatic sequence:

West	North	East	South
		1♡	pass
4♡	5◊	5♡	pass
pass	dbl	all pass	

I lead the ◊2 and this dummy is tabled:

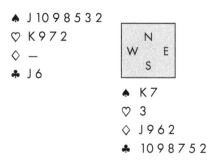

♠ J 10 9 8 5 3 2
♡ K 9 7 2
◊ —
♣ J 6

♠ K 7
♡ 3
◊ J 9 6 2
♣ 10 9 8 7 5 2

Declarer takes partner's queen with the ace, discarding one of dummy's clubs, and plays the ♠Q. I win with the king and belatedly switch to the ♣10, partner winning with the king and playing a second diamond. Declarer ruffs in dummy, ruffs a spade, plays a heart to dummy's nine and ruffs a third spade, removing partner's ace. A heart to the king gives access to the remaining spade winners.

This was the layout:

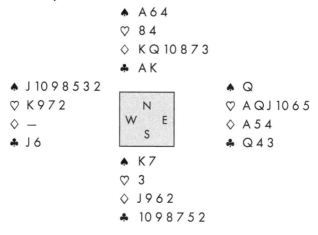

```
                      ♠ A 6 4
                      ♡ 8 4
                      ◇ K Q 10 8 7 3
                      ♣ A K
  ♠ J 10 9 8 5 3 2                      ♠ Q
  ♡ K 9 7 2            N                ♡ A Q J 10 6 5
  ◇ —              W       E            ◇ A 5 4
  ♣ J 6                S                ♣ Q 4 3
                      ♠ K 7
                      ♡ 3
                      ◇ J 9 6 2
                      ♣ 10 9 8 7 5 2
```

POST-MORTEM

In this type of situation, where a player has shown a long suit, it is unlikely that they will have doubled expecting to take many tricks in their suit. Had South led a black card (the ♠K now looks a good bet) it should not be difficult for the defenders to cash out.

In the other room, East saw fit to double 5◇. Leading the ♠Q would have given the defenders a chance — East can get in with the ◇A and underlead his ♡A to secure a spade ruff — but starting with the ♡A removed West's potential entry and meant there was a double game swing.

Andrew Robson's Bridge Club in London's Parson's Green is justifiably popular and attracts players from every level. During a matchpointed event there, I pick up these cards as South:

Dealer East.	♠ A 6
E-W Vul.	♡ K Q 9 8
	◇ Q 9 5 4
	♣ 10 4 3

The player to my left opens 1♡; when his partner responds 1♠, he jumps to 3♠ and is raised to game. This has been the brief auction:

West	North	East	South
		1♡	pass
1♠	pass	3♠	pass
4♠	all pass		

My partner leads the ◇J:

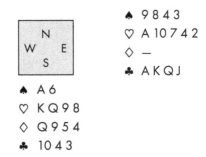

```
                              ♠ 9 8 4 3
                              ♡ A 10 7 4 2
            N                 ◇ —
         W     E              ♣ A K Q J
            S
        ♠ A 6
        ♡ K Q 9 8
        ◇ Q 9 5 4
        ♣ 10 4 3
```

Declarer ruffs in dummy and plays the ♠9. When I play the six, he lets the nine run and partner wins with the jack and returns the ♡J. Declarer wins with dummy's ace and plays four rounds of clubs, pitching the ♡6. My partner ruffs with the ♠7 and plays a heart, but the bird has flown, declarer ruffing and playing a second round of trumps, which sees the ace and king collide.

This was the full deal:

```
                    ♠ K J 7
                    ♡ J 3
                    ◇ J 10 7 6 3
                    ♣ 9 6 2
    ♠ Q 10 5 2                      ♠ 9 8 4 3
    ♡ 6 5              N            ♡ A 10 7 4 2
    ◇ A K 8 2      W     E          ◇ —
    ♣ 8 7 5           S            ♣ A K Q J
                    ♠ A 6
                    ♡ K Q 9 8
                    ◇ Q 9 5 4
                    ♣ 10 4 3
```

POST-MORTEM

With such a powerful dummy on display it should have been clear to South that he would need partner to have a strong holding in the trump suit. The reader may be ahead of me here when I reveal that the winning defense is for South to rise with the ♠A at Trick 2. After that, continuing with a spade, switching to the ♡K or even returning a club will leave declarer with only nine tricks. If declarer tries cashing the clubs as before, then South can ruff in with the ♠6.

17 | WHEN YOU HAVE ELIMINATED THE IMPOSSIBLE...

Many sports now offer competitions for 'senior' players and bridge is no exception. During a Senior team trial I pick up these average cards as South:

Dealer West.　　♠ J 9 3 2
Both Vul.　　　♡ Q 6
　　　　　　　♢ Q 4 3
　　　　　　　♣ K Q 10 6

When the player on my left opens 1♣ my partner has nothing to say, and after East responds 1♢, West rebids 1♡. East's next move is to bid 2♠, which is explained as 'forcing to game, but denying four spades'. When West continues with 2NT, East concludes the auction by raising to 3NT.

West	North	East	South
1♣	pass	1♢	pass
1♡	pass	2♠ *	pass
2NT	pass	3NT	all pass

My partner leads a fourth-best ♠6:

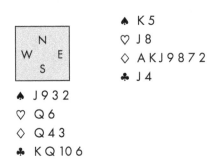

　　　　　　　　　♠ K 5
　　　　　　　　　♡ J 8
　　　　　　　　　♢ A K J 9 8 7 2
　　　　　　　　　♣ J 4

　　♠ J 9 3 2
　　♡ Q 6
　　♢ Q 4 3
　　♣ K Q 10 6

Declarer plays low from dummy, wins in hand with the ♠A and continues with the ♢6 to the ten, jack and my queen. When I return a spade declarer wins in dummy, cashes the diamonds and then plays on hearts, claiming the rest when my queen appears on the second round.

This was the full layout:

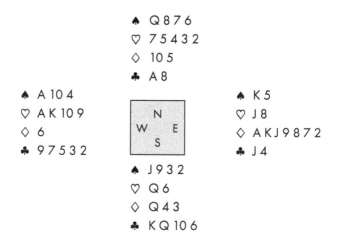

POST-MORTEM

With declarer having taken one trick and with seven more in clear view, it should have been obvious that the defenders needed to find four more tricks in a hurry. The only hope of doing that is to switch to the ♣6.

They managed that at the other table.

Although the number of entries continues to fall, English knockout events like the Gold Cup are always keenly contested. In 2007 the English Bridge Union introduced an inter-club event, and my old club has induced me to come out of semi-retirement in the somewhat dubious belief that this will increase their chances. My partner is an occasionally brilliant player who has represented his country on more than one occasion. Having survived the early rounds, we have reached the business end of the competition when I pick up this depressing hand as South:

Dealer East.	♠ J 5 4
Neither Vul.	♡ 9 5
	♦ J 10 9 7 6 4
	♣ 9 3

East opens 1♡ and, after West responds 1♠, my partner enters the fray with a double. When East bids 4♡, I venture 5♦. That does not deter West, who now jumps to 6♡, which my partner doubles, ending an exciting auction:

West	North	East	South
		1♡	pass
1♠	dbl	4♡	5♦
6♡	dbl	all pass	

I doubt partner is doubling in the hope of taking tricks in diamonds, as West's unforced jump to slam suggests he has the diamond suit under control. Despite the fact that it may give up a vital tempo, I decide to pay homage to David Bird's trump-leading Brother Hubert and place the ♡5 on the table:

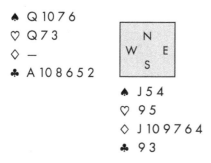

♠ Q 10 7 6
♡ Q 7 3
◇ —
♣ A 10 8 6 5 2

♠ J 5 4
♡ 9 5
◇ J 10 9 7 6 4
♣ 9 3

Declarer plays low from dummy and, when my partner discards the ♠2, he wins in hand with the ♡6. Now he plays the ♣Q to the ace, ruffs a club, ruffs a diamond and ruffs a third club high as I discard a diamond. Declarer's next move is to play the ♠3, and when I follow with the four he puts in dummy's ten. Partner wins with the king, and after some thought exits with the ◇3. Declarer wins with the queen, ruffs a diamond, ruffs a spade high and claims the rest.

The full deal looked like this:

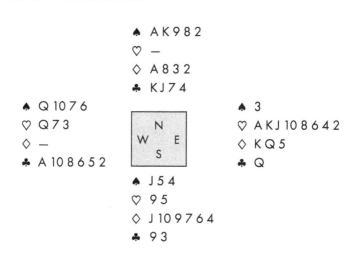

♠ A K 9 8 2
♡ —
◇ A 8 3 2
♣ K J 7 4

♠ Q 10 7 6
♡ Q 7 3
◇ —
♣ A 10 8 6 5 2

♠ 3
♡ A K J 10 8 6 4 2
◇ K Q 5
♣ Q

♠ J 5 4
♡ 9 5
◇ J 10 9 7 6 4
♣ 9 3

This was the position after partner had won the ♠K:

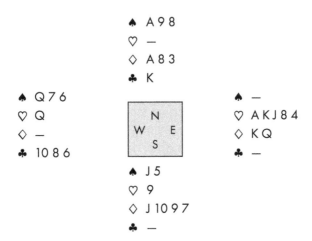

North had no good move. A club would allow declarer to ruff high, cross to dummy with the ♡Q and discard two diamonds on the established clubs. The ♠A would see declarer ruff, establishing dummy's queen, which would then take care of one of declarer's diamonds after the other had been ruffed.

I can prevent this by discarding a spade rather than a diamond on the third club. Then partner would be able to exit with the ♠A. Declarer can ruff, ruff a diamond and throw a diamond on the ♠Q, but I can ruff that with the ♡9.

Declarer can do better — after ruffing one club, a spade to the ten endplays North. Now, exiting with a club allows the suit to be established, while playing a spade or diamond is no better.

In the other room, the defender holding my cards made no mistake, pitching a spade on the third round of clubs. That left declarer with no hope other than the ruffing finesse in diamonds, so North scored his aces.

USE THE FORCE, LUKE...

19

In recent years there has been some debate about the merits of making a short-suit lead against a suit contract, especially where the defender has four trumps, as opposed to the traditional approach of adopting a forcing defense. During an all-too-rare outing at the club, I pick up as South:

Dealer North.	♠ 8
N-S Vul.	♡ K Q 6 3 2
	◇ K Q 9 7 2
	♣ 5 4

When partner opens 1♣ (natural with a weak notrump or any 18+), East overcalls 1♠ and I bid 2♡. West raises to 2♠ and my partner bids 3♡. East now raises the ante by bidding 4♠. If I decide to bid on then 5◇ is an obvious choice, as it may help partner should East-West go on to 5♠. However, there is nothing to suggest that we can take eleven tricks so I decide to indicate my extra values by doubling, which leaves us with this auction:

West	North	East	South
	1♣	1♠	2♡
2♠	3♡	4♠	dbl
all pass			

I am tempted to lead the ♣5, but as partner may have four trumps I start with the ♡K, which reveals this dummy:

♠ J 7 3
♡ 10 8 7 4
◇ J 10
♣ K 9 8 7

	N	
W		E
	S	

♠ 8
♡ K Q 6 3 2
◇ K Q 9 7 2
♣ 5 4

Partner follows with the nine and declarer the five. When I continue with the ♡3, declarer ruffs partner's jack and plays the ◊5. I go up with the queen, partner playing the ◊4, and exit with the ♡6, declarer ruffing partner's ace and continuing with the ◊6. When I play low, partner wins with the ace and returns the ◊3. Declarer throws the ♣10 from his hand, ruffs in dummy and plays the ♠J, covered by the king and ace, and continues with the ♣J, which he overtakes with dummy's king. His next move is to play dummy's ♣7 and run it. When it holds he plays a spade to the nine, cashes the ♠A and claims.

This was the layout:

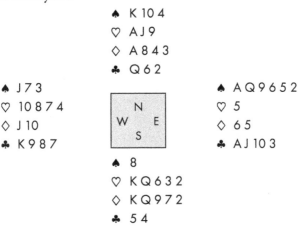

	♠ K 10 4	
	♡ A J 9	
	◊ A 8 4 3	
	♣ Q 6 2	
♠ J 7 3		♠ A Q 9 6 5 2
♡ 10 8 7 4		♡ 5
◊ J 10		◊ 6 5
♣ K 9 8 7		♣ A J 10 3
	♠ 8	
	♡ K Q 6 3 2	
	◊ K Q 9 7 2	
	♣ 5 4	

POST-MORTEM

Declarer's play was faultless but I missed an opportunity. If I win the second diamond with the king and play a fourth heart, declarer is forced to ruff and does not have the entries to avoid a black-suit loser.

In the other room they also played in 4♠ doubled, but declarer lost his way and finished three down!

THE WRONG SPOTS

20

Reaching the final of a major teams event is always exciting. My partner and opponents are of the highest caliber and I pick up these cards as South:

Dealer East.
Both Vul.

♠ Q 9
♡ K 9 8 7
◇ 9 6 4
♣ J 8 6 3

East opens a 15-17 1NT and, when West responds 2♣, his 2◇ denies a four-card major. West rebids 2♠, described as a mild game invitation. East is happy to accept, leaving us with this auction:

West	North	East	South
		1NT	pass
2♣	pass	2◇	pass
2♠ *	pass	4♠	all pass

My partner leads the ♣5 and dummy has nothing to spare for his bidding:

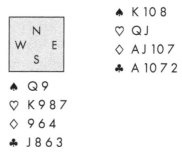

♠ K 10 8
♡ Q J
◇ A J 10 7
♣ A 10 7 2

♠ Q 9
♡ K 9 8 7
◇ 9 6 4
♣ J 8 6 3

Declarer plays dummy's two. When I contribute the ♣6, he wins with the king and plays the ♠2 to the five, ten and my queen. There is little point in continuing with a club so I switch to the ♡7 and am pleased to see partner win with the ace. When he switches to the ◇3 declarer plays low from dummy, wins with the queen, cashes the ♣Q, plays a diamond to dummy's jack and proceeds to discard two hearts on the minor-suit aces.

Not a triumph for our side when you see the full deal:

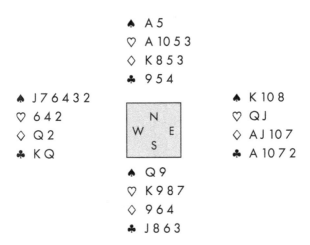

```
                    ♠ A 5
                    ♡ A 10 5 3
                    ◇ K 8 5 3
                    ♣ 9 5 4
  ♠ J 7 6 4 3 2            N          ♠ K 10 8
  ♡ 6 4 2            W         E      ♡ Q J
  ◇ Q 2                   S           ◇ A J 10 7
  ♣ K Q                               ♣ A 10 7 2
                    ♠ Q 9
                    ♡ K 9 8 7
                    ◇ 9 6 4
                    ♣ J 8 6 3
```

POST-MORTEM

One of the secrets of good defense is to make life as simple as possible for partner. The play in the spade suit strongly suggested that North held the ♠A, so finding partner with the ♡A was the best chance to defeat the contract.

Unfortunately, North was uncertain about the location of the ♡K and felt that the only way to defeat the contract was to find me with the ◇Q. On reflection, as I could be virtually certain that unless partner held the ♡A the contract could not be defeated, I should have returned the ♡K!

Declarer might have played a spade to the king — that caters for a singleton queen with South, but also takes into account the fact that North is unlikely to have ♠AQx. With that holding he can rise with the ace and play three rounds of hearts, forcing dummy to ruff and promoting a trick for the ♠Q. That defense also works when South has the singleton ♠A — after three rounds of hearts North's ♠Qx will be worth a second trick even though the ten draws the ace.

In the other room, after an identical start to the auction, East declined West's invitation. North led a diamond. Declarer won with the queen, unblocked the clubs, played a diamond to the ten and discarded two hearts on dummy's aces.

THE WEAKEST LINK

21

In his homage to rubber bridge, The Big Game, Robert Sheehan points out that if you are sitting at the table and can't work out who the weakest player is, then it's you! In the final of a major event I find myself surrounded by world champions when I pick up as South:

Dealer South.	♠ 8 5 3
N-S Vul.	♡ A K 9
	◇ A 10 6 4
	♣ K Q 6

Relieved to have a straightforward-looking hand, I open 1NT and my partner responds 2◇, a transfer to hearts. I dutifully bid 2♡, but when partner passes, East comes to life with a double. Holding a near maximum with good support for partner's suit I redouble; when West has nothing to say, East bids 3◇. I'm tempted to double that, but recalling England's Keith Stanley who politely enquired of a teammate who had conceded -470, 'Did you need the extra 50 points?', I keep my powder dry, leaving us with this auction:

West	North	East	South
			1NT
pass	2◇*	pass	2♡
pass	pass	dbl	redbl
pass	pass	3◇	all pass

I lead the ♡K and dummy is hardly terrifying:

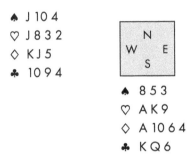

♠ J 10 4
♡ J 8 3 2
◇ K J 5
♣ 10 9 4

N
W   E
S

♠ 8 5 3
♡ A K 9
◇ A 10 6 4
♣ K Q 6

Partner follows with the four, confirming a five-card suit, and declarer plays the queen. I consider switching to the ♣Q (in our methods that would ask for attitude) but that risks declarer having the ♣AJ. Leading a trump might give up a trick in the suit and a spade can only help declarer, so eventually I decide to continue with a mildly deceptive ♡9. Declarer puts up dummy's jack and discards the ♠9 as partner follows with the ♡5. Declarer's next move is to play dummy's ♠J, and when partner follows with the six he plays the king, followed by the ◇3 to dummy's king, partner contributing the ◇2.

Declarer now plays dummy's ♣10 to my queen, partner playing the ♣3, and I exit with the ♡A, declarer ruffing and advancing the ◇8. When I play low he plays dummy's five and partner discards the ♣7. These cards remain:

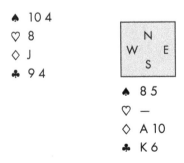

♠ 10 4
♡ 8
◇ J
♣ 9 4

N
W   E
S

♠ 8 5
♡ —
◇ A 10
♣ K 6

When declarer plays the ♣J, I attempt to reconstruct his hand. I know he started with one heart and five diamonds, and partner's play in clubs suggests he started with three cards in the suit, which means declarer must be 3=1=5=4. I know declarer has the ♠K, ♡Q, ◊Q and ♣J. Even if declarer has the ♠A his hand would still be quite modest for the balancing double, so I am inclined to place him with the ♣A as well. Not wanting to appear foolish, I go up with the ♣K, and when partner's card proves to be the ace I can feel my neck changing color. Partner continues with the ♡10 and when declarer ruffs with the ◊Q I overruff, at which point declarer claims the rest.

Regrettably, I have to reveal the full deal:

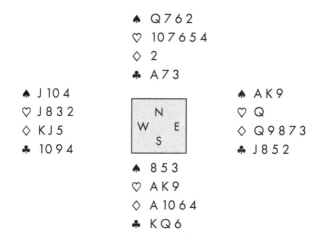

```
              ♠ Q 7 6 2
              ♡ 10 7 6 5 4
              ◊ 2
              ♣ A 7 3
  ♠ J 10 4                    ♠ A K 9
  ♡ J 8 3 2       N           ♡ Q
  ◊ K J 5      W     E        ◊ Q 9 8 7 3
  ♣ 10 9 4        S           ♣ J 8 5 2
              ♠ 8 5 3
              ♡ A K 9
              ◊ A 10 6 4
              ♣ K Q 6
```

POST-MORTEM

We could have defeated the contract several times over — and by more than one trick. Although I got the distribution right, I failed to ask myself what declarer might have done holding ♠AK9 ♡Q ◊Q9873 ♣AJ52 — with that hand he might have bid 2♡ over partner's 2◊ as a takeout maneuver. Had partner discarded a heart or spade rather than a club, the clubs would not have crashed, but even at the end I could have defeated the contract by refusing to overruff the ◊Q.

I ruefully recall the adage, 'If wishes were horses, then beggars would ride'.

Playing in trials for the European Pairs Championships, my partner is a sound performer. We are comfortably placed when, towards the end of the event, I find myself looking at this hand as South:

Dealer East.
N-S Vul.

♠ J 5 2
♡ Q 6
♢ J 6
♣ K 10 8 7 5 4

East opens 1♡ and when West responds 1♠, his rebid of 1NT (promising 11-14) is raised to game. That gives us this routine auction:

West	North	East	South
		1♡	pass
1♠	pass	1NT*	pass
3NT	all pass		

I lead the ♣7 and dummy appears:

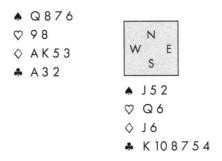

♠ Q 8 7 6
♡ 9 8
♢ A K 5 3
♣ A 3 2

♠ J 5 2
♡ Q 6
♢ J 6
♣ K 10 8 7 5 4

Declarer plays low from dummy, taking partner's jack with the queen. A diamond to the ace is followed by the ♡9, which runs to my queen as partner plays the ♡3. The ♡2 is missing, and since declarer would have rebid a six-card suit I can place partner with four hearts. When I continue with the ♣K, declarer goes up with dummy's ace. Now he plays the ♡8, overtakes it with the ♡10 and cashes the ace. When I discard a club, declarer exits with a heart and partner wins with the king and returns the ♢Q. When declarer withholds dummy's ace, these cards remain:

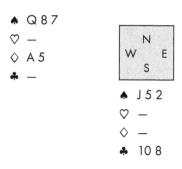

♠ Q 8 7
♡ —
◇ A 5
♣ —

♠ J 5 2
♡ —
◇ —
♣ 10 8

When partner continues with the ◇10, declarer wins with dummy's ace and exits with the ◇5. Forced to win with the seven, my partner has to play a spade. Declarer runs that to dummy's queen, crosses to hand with the ♠A and takes the game-going trick with the ♡5.

This was the full deal:

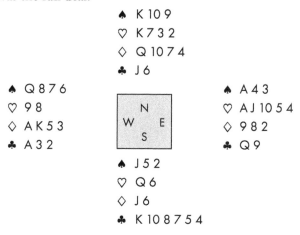

♠ K 10 9
♡ K 7 3 2
◇ Q 10 7 4
♣ J 6

♠ Q 8 7 6
♡ 9 8
◇ A K 5 3
♣ A 3 2

♠ A 4 3
♡ A J 10 5 4
◇ 9 8 2
♣ Q 9

♠ J 5 2
♡ Q 6
◇ J 6
♣ K 10 8 7 5 4

POST-MORTEM

Had declarer ducked the ♣K, a spade or diamond switch would have been good enough. However, unless declarer has rebid 1NT with a singleton ♣Q, my partner can hold only two clubs, so with no obvious entry in my hand there is no future in the suit. If I switch to a spade, partner puts in the nine and, if declarer ducks, he can exit with a club. If declarer wins and plays on hearts as before, my partner should be able to find the play of exiting with a diamond, which holds declarer to eight tricks.

Despite the fact that I have always considered myself to be a modest card-holder at the rubber-bridge table, I find it difficult to resist the odd invitation to take part in a high-stakes session. For once I am in the plus column when I pick up these cards as South:

Dealer West. ♠ K 8 5
E-W Vul. ♡ Q 8 5
 ◇ A 10 9 8
 ♣ Q 5 2

West opens 1♣ and my partner overcalls 2♣, promising a hand with both majors. When East raises to 3♣ I decide to compete with 4♣, which invites partner to choose a major. When West jumps to 6♣, partner rejects my invitation, leaving this sequence:

West	North	East	South
1♣	2♣ *	3♣	4♣ *
6♣	all pass		

My partner leads the ♡J:

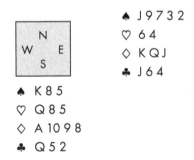

 ♠ J 9 7 3 2
 ♡ 6 4
 ◇ K Q J
 ♣ J 6 4

 ♠ K 8 5
 ♡ Q 8 5
 ◇ A 10 9 8
 ♣ Q 5 2

Declarer wins with the ♡A and plays the ◇5 to dummy's jack, my partner following with the seven. My partner would have led a singleton diamond, so after winning with the ace I return a heart. Declarer produces the king and cashes the ♣A, partner following with the seven. Declarer now plays the ♡7, ruffing it in dummy, ruffs a spade, crosses to dummy with a diamond and ruffs another spade. Entering dummy for a third time with a diamond, he ruffs another spade and then ruffs his last diamond. Dummy is down to the ♠J9, and when declarer calls for the jack my ♣Q5 are caught by declarer's ♣K10.

This was how the cards were disposed:

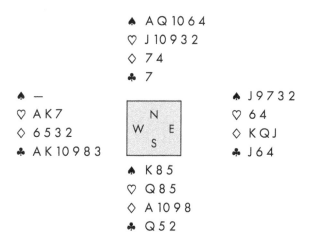

```
                    ♠ A Q 10 6 4
                    ♡ J 10 9 3 2
                    ◇ 7 4
                    ♣ 7
  ♠ —                                 ♠ J 9 7 3 2
  ♡ A K 7            N                ♡ 6 4
  ◇ 6 5 3 2      W       E            ◇ K Q J
  ♣ A K 10 9 8 3     S                ♣ J 6 4
                    ♠ K 8 5
                    ♡ Q 8 5
                    ◇ A 10 9 8
                    ♣ Q 5 2
```

POST-MORTEM

Declarer's play was faultless, but mine was capable of improvement. If I withhold the ◇A on the first round of the suit, declarer is left without resource. If he ruffs a spade and plays a second diamond, I can win and give partner a diamond ruff. If declarer tries to prevent this by playing a round of trumps, I can play a second trump and again there will only be eleven tricks.

The defensive duck is hard to find, but can frequently be the best line of defense. Suppose on this deal dummy's diamonds were ◇AQJ with South holding ◇K1098. Now the strongest defense is to withhold the ◇K when declarer takes the finesse. If declarer subsequently repeats the finesse, South can win and will always have a winning move available.

It was an expensive mistake.

Long matchpointed events test one's concentration to the limit, as every deal may contain a hidden booby-trap. My partner was highly thought of as a junior, but then turned his hand to business. Returning to the game after making his millions, he is established as one of the top seniors, although he likes to go his own way in the bidding. I find myself, as South, looking at:

Dealer West.   ♠ J 10 5
Neither Vul.   ♡ 8
                  ◇ Q 9 8 3
                  ♣ A K 8 7 2

When West starts with a strong 1NT, the auction does not last long; East transfers to hearts with 2◇ and then jumps to 3NT, West going back to 4♡.

West	North	East	South
1NT	pass	2◇	pass
2♡	pass	3NT	pass
4♡	all pass		

My partner leads the ♡4 and dummy's major asset proves to be the trump suit:

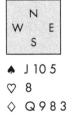

                        ♠ 7 3 2
                        ♡ A K Q J 7
                        ◇ 10 6 4
                        ♣ J 5

          ♠ J 10 5
          ♡ 8
          ◇ Q 9 8 3
          ♣ A K 8 7 2

Declarer wins with dummy's ace and plays a spade. When I follow with the five, he plays the nine; partner wins with the king and continues with the ♡5. Declarer wins in dummy, and plays a third round of hearts, partner following with the ten as I discard two clubs. His next move is to play dummy's ♣J. I win with the king, declarer following with the six and partner the four.

Declarer must have most of the missing high cards, but I don't think he has the ◊J, as then he might have taken a diamond finesse. As to his shape, I am inclined to place him with 4-4 in the majors, since with a 3=4=3=3 pattern there would have been a good case for passing 3NT.

Although I doubt it will matter, I postpone cashing my second club trick and exit with the ♠J. Declarer wins with the ace, cashes the queen and then produces the ♠4. On this trick partner catastrophically discards the ◊2; declarer now overtakes the ♡9 with dummy's jack and plays the last heart in this position:

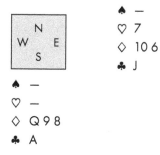

```
                              ♠  —
                              ♡  7
        N                     ◊  10 6
     W     E                  ♣  J
        S
  ♠  —
  ♡  —
  ◊  Q 9 8
  ♣  A
```

Forced to retain the ♣A, I have to part with a diamond; declarer throws the ♣Q and scores the last three tricks in diamonds.

This was the layout:

                    ♠ K 8 6
                    ♡ 10 5 4
                    ◇ J 7 2
                    ♣ 10 9 4 3
    ♠ A Q 9 4   ♠ 7 3 2
    ♡ 9 6 3 2   ♡ A K Q J 7
    ◇ A K 5   ◇ 10 6 4
    ♣ Q 6   ♣ J 5
                    ♠ J 10 5
                    ♡ 8
                    ◇ Q 9 8 3
                    ♣ A K 8 7 2

POST-MORTEM

Good defense involves making life simple for partner, so although North's discard of the ◇2 was an error, the real mistake was mine in not cashing the second club.

This is the difficulty of matchpoints — every trick is vital; at IMPs our slips would hardly have cost.

Board-a-match events are strenuous. Even though it is often the case that a point is lost irretrievably as a result of what happens at one table, there is no way of knowing this, and one must fight tooth and nail for every trick. Reflecting that in the Reisinger final there are no easy encounters, I find myself looking at these South cards:

Dealer East.	♠	K J 4
Neither Vul.	♡	Q 6 5 3 2
	◇	A 6
	♣	A 5 3

When East opens 1♡, West responds with 2♠, which is described as promising invitational values. When East declines the invitation, we are left with this auction:

West	North	East	South
		1♡	pass
2♠*	all pass		

North leads the ◇K:

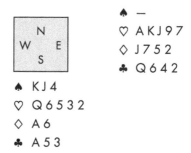

	♠	—
	♡	A K J 9 7
	◇	J 7 5 2
	♣	Q 6 4 2

	♠	K J 4
	♡	Q 6 5 3 2
	◇	A 6
	♣	A 5 3

When I allow the ◇K to hold, my partner continues with the ◇8. Declarer ruffs with the ♠2, cashes the ♠A and follows it with the ♠5. I win with the jack and, knowing from my partner's play in diamonds that he has no interest in clubs, I exit with the ♡5. Declarer wins in hand with the

♡10 and plays a third spade. I take the king and return the ♡2. Partner ruffs that with the ♠10, but the ♣A proves to be our last defensive trick.

This was the complete deal:

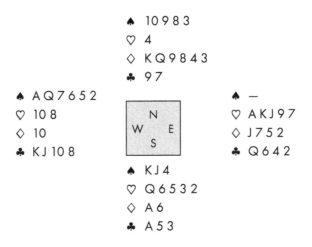

```
                    ♠ 10 9 8 3
                    ♡ 4
                    ◇ K Q 9 8 4 3
                    ♣ 9 7
    ♠ A Q 7 6 5 2                        ♠ —
    ♡ 10 8              N                ♡ A K J 9 7
    ◇ 10          W          E           ◇ J 7 5 2
    ♣ K J 10 8            S              ♣ Q 6 4 2
                    ♠ K J 4
                    ♡ Q 6 5 3 2
                    ◇ A 6
                    ♣ A 5 3
```

POST-MORTEM

I was right to switch to hearts, but the correct card was the ♡Q! That locks declarer in dummy. If he plays a club, I can rise with the ace and give partner a heart ruff. When North returns a diamond, I will ruff with the ♠K and lead another heart, promoting the ♠10 into the setting trick.

Declarer would have done better to retain a degree of control in the trump suit by leading a low spade at Trick 3. If I win that and play the ♡Q, he can win in dummy and play a club, and will subsequently be able to play ace and another spade.

The defense might have been easier if North had led his singleton heart. If declarer wins in dummy and plays a club, South can duck and will be able to give North two ruffs — one in hearts and one in clubs.

In the other room West responded 1NT, promising five or more spades, and when East (perhaps constrained by system) rebid 2◇, he continued with 3♣, the resulting 3NT finishing four down.

LEADING QUESTION

26

Playing in a big board-a-match teams final, I pick up these cards as South:

Dealer North.	♠ Q 8 7 6
Both Vul.	♡ Q 10 3
	◇ Q J 9 6
	♣ 8 5

When East opens 1♣, West responds 1♠ and then introduces the fourth suit with 2♡ over East's 2◇ rebid. He raises the reply of 2NT to game, leaving us with this simple sequence:

West	North	East	South
	pass	1♣	pass
1♠	pass	2◇	pass
2♡*	pass	2NT	pass
3NT	all pass		

West's use of the fourth suit suggest that he does not have a heart stopper himself, so with East marked with five clubs and four diamonds there is no reason to look beyond the heart suit. I start with the ♡3:

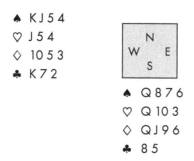

♠ K J 5 4
♡ J 5 4
◇ 10 5 3
♣ K 7 2

♠ Q 8 7 6
♡ Q 10 3
◇ Q J 9 6
♣ 8 5

Declarer thinks for a while and then puts up dummy's jack. Partner covers with the king and declarer wins with the ace and plays the ♠10, covered by the queen, king and ace. Partner returns a heart, but after cashing the ten and queen I have no way to put partner in and declarer takes nine tricks.

The full deal:

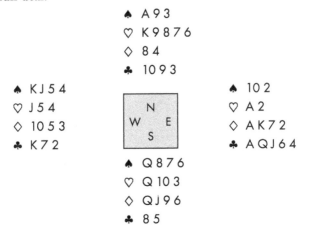

```
                    ♠ A 9 3
                    ♡ K 9 8 7 6
                    ◇ 8 4
                    ♣ 10 9 3
  ♠ K J 5 4                           ♠ 10 2
  ♡ J 5 4           N                 ♡ A 2
  ◇ 10 5 3       W     E              ◇ A K 7 2
  ♣ K 7 2           S                 ♣ A Q J 6 4
                    ♠ Q 8 7 6
                    ♡ Q 10 3
                    ◇ Q J 9 6
                    ♣ 8 5
```

POST-MORTEM

I was right to lead a heart, but in this type of situation it is frequently best to start with the ♡10, which avoids blocking the suit.

In the replay, my counterpart also led the ♡3 but declarer missed the blocking play, winning the trick with the ace and cashing five rounds of clubs. North played the ♣9 on the first round, followed by the three and ten, and South pitched the ◇6. On the penultimate club, South, worried about the spade suit, parted with the ◇9 and now declarer was up to ten tricks, enough to win the point.

Suppose instead North plays his clubs in the order ♣10, ♣9, ♣3. That should suggest he has spades under control.

One final point — North might have doubled 2♡.

A Singular Point

27

Some team events start with a number of qualifying rounds leading up to a series of knockout matches. Playing in one of the best Polish events, we have strengthened our team with some of the many experts from Bulgaria, while my partner has already won a European Pairs title. During one of the knockout matches against first-class opposition, I pick up this average hand as South:

Dealer North.	♠ Q 5 4 3
N-S Vul.	♡ J 10 4 2
	◇ 10 7 4
	♣ A K

East's opening bid of 2NT, promising 20-21 points, is raised to game, giving this brief auction:

West	North	East	South
	pass	2NT	pass
3NT	all pass		

At best partner will have 5-6 points, so the opening lead may have a significant role to play. A spade may work well when partner has the ace and the suit is 4-3-3-3 around the table. A heart is more likely to be successful when partner has a smattering of points, perhaps the ♡Q or ♡K and a useful defensive card somewhere else. A diamond is totally passive — and that would be very much in the modern style — but it risks giving away a tempo. I could cash a club and then decide how to continue, but that is not without risk.

Eventually a memory stirs and, recalling a theory advanced by the celebrated English twins, Bob and Jim Sharples, that with an equal choice between the majors one should lead a heart, I place the ♡2 on the table:

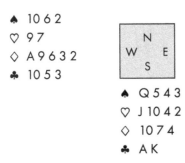

```
    ♠ 10 6 2
    ♡ 9 7
    ◇ A 9 6 3 2
    ♣ 10 5 3
                    ♠ Q 5 4 3
                    ♡ J 10 4 2
                    ◇ 10 7 4
                    ♣ A K
```

When partner plays the ♡Q and declarer ducks, it appears I have struck gold. Declarer ducks partner's ♡K on the next round and then takes the ♡8 with the ace, discarding a club from dummy. He then cashes the ◇KQ, overtakes the ◇J with dummy's ace and cashes two more tricks in the suit, throwing a heart and the ♣9 from his hand. Partner discards the ♣2, the ♠8 and the ♣4, while I part with the ♠4.

With me still to play to dummy's last diamond, these cards remain:

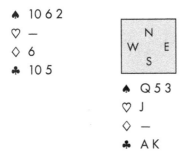

```
    ♠ 10 6 2
    ♡ —
    ◇ 6
    ♣ 10 5
                    ♠ Q 5 3
                    ♡ J
                    ◇ —
                    ♣ A K
```

Not wanting to give up one of my winners, I part with the ♠3 and that proves to be disastrous, as you can see from the full deal:

```
                    ♠ J 9 8
                    ♡ K Q 8
                    ◇ 8 5
                    ♣ 8 7 6 4 2
     ♠ 10 6 2                          ♠ A K 7
     ♡ 9 7            N                ♡ A 6 5 3
     ◇ A 9 6 3 2    W     E            ◇ K Q J
     ♣ 10 5 3          S               ♣ Q J 9
                    ♠ Q 5 4 3
                    ♡ J 10 4 2
                    ◇ 10 7 4
                    ♣ A K
```

POST-MORTEM

At the point where I pitched a second spade, the winning defense was to throw the ♡J. That relies on partner holding the ♠J, but if declarer has that card (getting him up to 21 points) then there is no defense, as if I part with a top club or a heart I can be thrown in with a club to lead into the spade tenace. Although the defense would have been easier if partner had retained all his spades, I should have got this right.

If you look closely, you will see that South can lead any one of the four suits and still defeat the contract, although some care will be needed depending on which suit is selected.

In recent years I have made an occasional foray into Mixed Pairs events. On deals where a post-mortem occurs, my present partner is fond of answering my question about her choice of action by replying, 'It's complicated'. On this deal my South hand is nothing special:

Dealer North.   ♠ K 4 3 2
Neither Vul.   ♡ K 8 4
                ◇ Q 5 4
                ♣ 8 3 2

When my partner passes, East opens 2NT (20-21) and West goes on to game. The brief auction:

West	North	East	South
	pass	2NT	pass
3NT	all pass		

Anything could be right here. In the modern style, I am tempted to start with a passive club, but given that the opponents have made no attempt to locate a major-suit fit I decide to lead the ♠2:

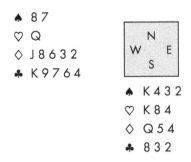

♠ 8 7
♡ Q
◇ J 8 6 3 2
♣ K 9 7 6 4

♠ K 4 3 2
♡ K 8 4
◇ Q 5 4
♣ 8 3 2

Partner covers dummy's ♠7 with the ten, and declarer wins with the queen and plays the ◇K. Partner takes that with the ace and returns the ♠J. Declarer wins with the ace and continues with the ◇10. I duck that, partner following with the seven, and when declarer produces the ♢9, I win with the queen as partner pitches the ♡2. These cards remain:

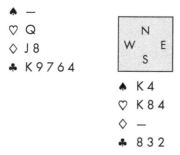

♠ —
♡ Q
♢ J 8
♣ K 9 7 6 4

♠ K 4
♡ K 8 4
♢ —
♣ 8 3 2

Unless partner is playing a very deep game, declarer has at least two spades left, including the nine. Declarer must have both the ♡A and the ♣A and presumably also the ♡J and the ♣Q to get up to 20 points. My best chance must be to hope declarer has a doubleton club, so I switch to the ♣2. When partner plays the ♣10, declarer wins in hand with the ace and plays the ♠9. I win that with the king and anxiously await partner's card. When it proves to be the six, declarer waits for my club return, goes up with dummy's king and claims nine tricks. This was the layout:

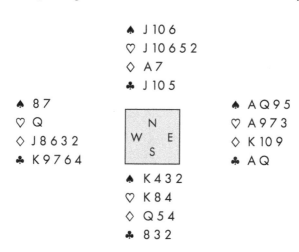

♠ J 10 6
♡ J 10 6 5 2
♢ A 7
♣ J 10 5

♠ 8 7
♡ Q
♢ J 8 6 3 2
♣ K 9 7 6 4

♠ A Q 9 5
♡ A 9 7 3
♢ K 10 9
♣ A Q

♠ K 4 3 2
♡ K 8 4
♢ Q 5 4
♣ 8 3 2

This is indeed a complicated deal, but we missed our way at several points. At Trick 2, partner might have ducked the ◇K on general principles. At Trick 4 (after a second round of diamonds) a spade continuation will see declarer win and play a third diamond, at which point I will need to find the spectacular play of the ♡K! A heart switch from partner at Trick 3 would have been a killer, but is hardly obvious.

Do you see why ducking the first diamond is important? If declarer, after winning the second spade, unblocks the clubs and then plays the ◇10, I have no answer — ducking allows declarer to win with dummy's jack and cash the clubs.

It is worth noting that even if declarer holds the ♡J, an initial club lead defeats the contract — as long as partner ducks the ◇K. When she does get in with the ◇A, a second club (or a low heart) will end declarer's hopes.

Meckwell

In the final of the Blue Ribbon Pairs, my partner enjoys the opportunity to compete with the best. The player on my left has a famous name not unconnected with a Law relating to six-card majors, while his equally famous partner is known for his comprehensive files.

> *Dealer South.*   ♠ J 8 3
> *Neither Vul.*   ♡ A 10 4 2
>   ◇ K Q 9
>   ♣ 10 3 2

I have nothing to say as dealer, and when the next two players also pass, East opens 1♣, promising 16 or more points. When I pass, West responds 1◇ showing 0-7 points and East rebids 1♠, which might be a four-card suit either in a three-suited hand or a hand with a long minor. West now bids 1NT, promising fewer than 6 or 7 points, but when East continues with 2NT he bids a natural 3♡ and East's 3NT concludes this scientific auction:

West	North	East	South
			pass
pass	pass	1♣*	pass
1◇*	pass	1♠*	pass
1NT*	pass	2NT	pass
3♡	pass	3NT	all pass

My partner leads a fourth-best ◊5 and East's hand proves to be the type with a long minor:

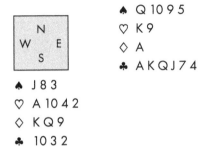

♠ Q 10 9 5
♡ K 9
◊ A
♣ A K Q J 7 4

♠ J 8 3
♡ A 10 4 2
◊ K Q 9
♣ 10 3 2

My partner's card more or less guarantees an honor and he might be leading from a suit headed by the ◊J10. To cater for that possibility, I unblock the ◊K under dummy's ace, declarer following with the four. Unsurprisingly, declarer now cashes dummy's clubs. Everyone follows to the first two rounds, and on the third one declarer throws the ♡5 and partner the ♠4. On the next club I discard the ♡4, declarer the ♡3 and partner the ♠2, confirming an even number of cards in that suit. On the penultimate club I pitch the ♡2, declarer the ♡6 and partner the ◊2. These cards remain:

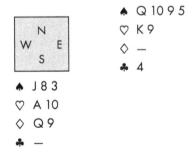

♠ Q 10 9 5
♡ K 9
◊ —
♣ 4

♠ J 8 3
♡ A 10
◊ Q 9
♣ —

I know partner's shape (4=2=5=2) and also that declarer cannot have the ♠AK. I don't think partner would discard a diamond holding ◊J10, so declarer must have one of those two cards. If it is the ◊J, I don't see how we can get up to five tricks. If partner has the ♠A, then unless I am very much mistaken, it is safe to pitch the ♡10. Even if declarer guesses to duck a heart to my ace, I will be able to cash the ◊Q and play the ◊9, trusting partner to have the ◊8. When I throw the ♡10, declarer matches it with the ♡7, and after some thought partner pitches the ♡Q. Realizing what has happened, declarer calls for dummy's ♡9 and my ace collects the ♡8 and partner's jack. I cash the ◇Q and follow it with the ◇9, covered by the ten and jack, and partner cashes the ◇8. Declarer discards dummy's ♡K on that and at Trick 12 my partner has to lead away from the ♠K into the split tenace.

This was the layout:

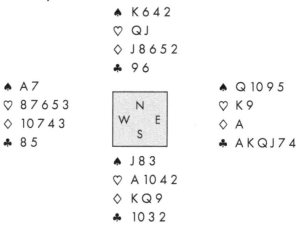

```
                    ♠ K 6 4 2
                    ♡ Q J
                    ◇ J 8 6 5 2
                    ♣ 9 6
  ♠ A 7                              ♠ Q 10 9 5
  ♡ 8 7 6 5 3          N             ♡ K 9
  ◇ 10 7 4 3       W       E         ◇ A
  ♣ 8 5                S             ♣ A K Q J 7 4
                    ♠ J 8 3
                    ♡ A 10 4 2
                    ◇ K Q 9
                    ♣ 10 3 2
```

POST-MORTEM

I was very much mistaken. This was the position when declarer played the last club:

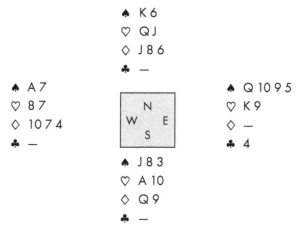

```
                    ♠ K 6
                    ♡ Q J
                    ◇ J 8 6
                    ♣ —
  ♠ A 7                              ♠ Q 10 9 5
  ♡ 8 7                N             ♡ K 9
  ◇ 10 7 4         W       E         ◇ —
  ♣ —                  S             ♣ 4
                    ♠ J 8 3
                    ♡ A 10
                    ◇ Q 9
                    ♣ —
```

After I pitched the ♡10, partner had no good move — a spade is hopeless, but if he parts with a diamond declarer can play two rounds of spades and will then only need to get the heart suit right. I could have avoided all danger by discarding a spade. Then when partner gets in with the ♠K, the ♡Q gives us the last four tricks.

However, declarer offered me a lifeline by ducking a heart (two rounds of spades sees dummy take the last trick with the ♠Q). Suppose after winning with the ♡A, I continue with the ◇9! If declarer covers, partner wins and plays back a diamond and now a spade switch is deadly. If declarer ducks the ◇9, I cash the queen and then play a spade.

Even if declarer has been dealt the ◇J then it is still possible for the defenders to prevail. South must keep three hearts, discarding two spades.

The Internet has brought many innovations to the world of bridge. One of them is the opportunity for thousands to compete at the same time in worldwide simultaneous events, such as those organized by Anna Gudge and Mark Newton through their EcatsBridge platform. During one of these events I hold these cards as South:

Dealer West.   ♠ K Q J 10 5
N-S Vul.   ♡ 8 5 4 2
               ◇ A 9 6
               ♣ 8

When West opens 1♣, East responds 1♡ and I overcall 1♠. When West rebids 3♣, East continues with 3♡ and I am surprised when that brings the auction to a close:

West	North	East	South
1♣	pass	1♡	1♠
3♣	pass	3♡	all pass

I lead the ♠K:

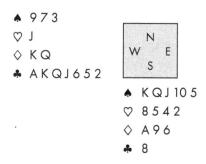

♠ 9 7 3
♡ J
◇ K Q
♣ A K Q J 6 5 2

        ♠ K Q J 10 5
        ♡ 8 5 4 2
        ◇ A 9 6
        ♣ 8

In an uncontested auction, East's 3♡ would be considered to be forcing. Here, West might have continued with 3♠, hoping East could deliver a spade stopper.

Partner overtakes the ♠K with the ace and returns the six. I win with the ten and cash the ♠J, on which partner discards the ◇5. It is clear that dummy's clubs will be able to take care of any losing diamonds in declarer's hand, so I cash the ◇A and then play a fourth spade. Declarer ruffs with dummy's ♡J, discarding a diamond from his hand, ruffs a diamond and draws trumps with the ♡AKQ10.

This was the full deal:

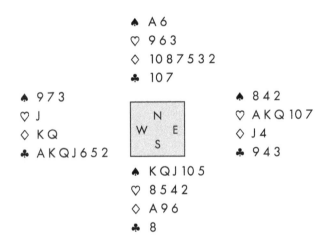

```
                    ♠ A 6
                    ♡ 9 6 3
                    ◇ 10 8 7 5 3 2
                    ♣ 10 7
    ♠ 9 7 3                         ♠ 8 4 2
    ♡ J               N             ♡ A K Q 10 7
    ◇ K Q         W       E         ◇ J 4
    ♣ A K Q J 6 5 2      S          ♣ 9 4 3
                    ♠ K Q J 10 5
                    ♡ 8 5 4 2
                    ◇ A 9 6
                    ♣ 8
```

POST-MORTEM

I should have played a fourth round of spades before cashing the ◇A. If declarer ruffs with dummy's ♡J and plays a diamond, I win and play my last spade and partner ruffs with the ♡9, promoting my ♡8 to the setting trick. If declarer discards from dummy on the fourth spade, partner ruffs with the ♡9 and trumps can no longer be drawn.

Bridge may be unique in that it is possible for anyone to play against the greatest champions. That is especially true in pairs events, but it can also happen in team contests at the highest level, as the Rosenblum Cup and McConnell Trophy are open to all-comers. With everyone playing the same deals, you sometimes get spectacular results. During the round-robin phase of the Rosenblum, I find myself looking at these cards as South:

Dealer North.	♠ 2
Neither Vul.	♡ 7 4
	◊ A Q J 9 8 7 6 3
	♣ 9 6

My partner opens 1NT, in this instance promising 10-12 points, and when East passes I must consider how best to respond. A tactical 3NT is one possibility. Another would be to transfer to diamonds via 2NT, which in our methods would allow me to discover if we have a good fit. Eventually I opt for a third alternative and jump to 5◊. After some consideration, West bids 5♡, which brings the auction to an end:

West	North	East	South
	1NT*	pass	5◊
5♡	all pass		

Partner leads the ♣K (asking me to give count) and dummy is revealed:

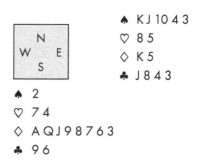

	♠ K J 10 4 3
	♡ 8 5
	◊ K 5
	♣ J 8 4 3
♠ 2	
♡ 7 4	
◊ A Q J 9 8 7 6 3	
♣ 9 6	

When I follow with the nine, partner continues with the ace and then plays the ♣5, declarer having followed with the two and seven. I ruff with the ♡4, but declarer overruffs with the six, draws trumps in three rounds and cashes the ♠A, claiming when everyone follows. This was the full deal:

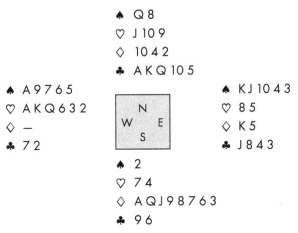

```
              ♠ Q 8
              ♡ J 10 9
              ◊ 10 4 2
              ♣ A K Q 10 5
♠ A 9 7 6 5                    ♠ K J 10 4 3
♡ A K Q 6 3 2      N           ♡ 8 5
◊ —             W     E        ◊ K 5
♣ 7 2              S           ♣ J 8 4 3
              ♠ 2
              ♡ 7 4
              ◊ A Q J 9 8 7 6 3
              ♣ 9 6
```

POST-MORTEM

If I had ruffed with the ♡7, it would have promoted one of partner's trumps. In situations like this it is invariably right to ruff as high as possible.

In the other room after an identical start, West decided to cuebid 6◊ on the first round and East bid 6♠. When South failed to lead a club, declarer took all the tricks.

Playing in a mixed event, the world champion on my left has a name not unconnected with the fashion industry. His partner is more of an unknown quantity. Mine is formidable, frequently being misattributed as inventor of a popular defense to 1NT. I find myself looking at a modest hand as South:

Dealer West.
E-W Vul.

♠ Q 8 6
♡ A 6 4 2
♢ 3 2
♣ Q 9 7 5

West opens 2♣ and rebids 2NT over his partner's negative response of 2♢. East now bids 3♡ as a transfer to spades and then raises her partner's 3♠ to game:

West	North	East	South
2♣*	pass	2♢*	pass
2NT	pass	3♡*	pass
3♠	pass	4♠	all pass

Partner leads the ◊10 and the first thing I notice is that dummy has a spade fewer than I expected:

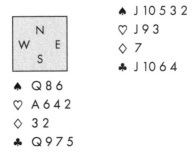

♠ J 10 5 3 2
♡ J 9 3
◊ 7
♣ J 10 6 4

♠ Q 8 6
♡ A 6 4 2
◊ 3 2
♣ Q 9 7 5

I follow with the three and declarer wins with the king and returns the ◊4, ruffing in dummy as partner follows with the six. Next comes the ♠2, covered in turn by the six, nine and ace. When partner continues with the ◊5, I ruff with the ♠8 and declarer follows with the jack. I switch to the ♣5 but declarer plays the ace, lays down the ♠K, collecting my queen and partner's four, and faces his hand. This was how the cards were distributed:

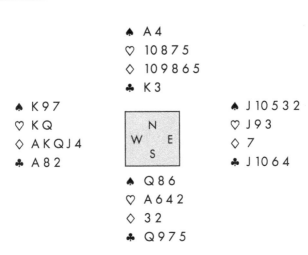

♠ A 4
♡ 10 8 7 5
◊ 10 9 8 6 5
♣ K 3

♠ K 9 7
♡ K Q
◊ A K Q J 4
♣ A 8 2

♠ J 10 5 3 2
♡ J 9 3
◊ 7
♣ J 10 6 4

♠ Q 8 6
♡ A 6 4 2
◊ 3 2
♣ Q 9 7 5

If my partner had switched to a heart or a club at Trick 3, declarer would have had no chance of ten tricks as long as in the former case I win and return a club. However, I missed an opportunity to give declarer a nudge in the wrong direction. I should ruff the third round of diamonds with the ♠Q, following the established principle of playing the card you are known to hold. When I switch to a club, declarer must win with the ace and will surely place North with the missing trumps.

If he draws trumps ending in hand, he can pitch dummy's remaining clubs on his two high diamonds, then knock out the ace of hearts. However, I can win the first heart and force dummy with a club: with the heart suit blocked, declarer will have to win the next heart in hand and lose a club in the ending.

In that scenario the solution would be to cash the master diamonds, pitching dummy's losing clubs as North follows helplessly and South discards (having no more trumps). Declarer then knocks out the ♡A, wins any return, unblocks the hearts, and draws trumps ending in dummy to enjoy the heart jack.

However, South will unexpectedly produce the ♠8 on the fourth round of diamonds and play a club (if North has the wit to drop the ♣K under the ace, South can cash the queen and give North a ruff for three down!).

The three annual American Nationals offer a feast of bridge and attract players from near and far. Warming up for the main events, we are contesting a single session board-a-match event when I pick up this modest hand as South:

> *Dealer North.*   ♠ 8 6 5
> *Neither Vul.*   ♡ K 8 3 2
>   ◇ Q 8 2
>   ♣ 10 7 4

My partner opens 1♠ and East doubles. I raise defensively to 2♠ and West bids 3◇. When my partner passes, East bids 3♠ and I pass, my partner alerting and explaining that it denies a high spade honor. When West bids 3NT my partner doubles, which ends the auction:

West	North	East	South
	1♠	dbl	2♠
3◇	pass	3♠*	pass*
3NT	dbl	all pass	

Partner leads a fourth-best ♠4 and when dummy is revealed, I see that my high cards might be well-placed:

```
              ♠ Q
              ♡ A J 10 4
      N       ◇ A J 10
   W     E    ♣ A 9 6 3 2
      S
   ♠ 8 6 5
   ♡ K 8 3 2
   ◇ Q 8 2
   ♣ 10 7 4
```

Dummy's queen takes the trick and declarer immediately advances the ◇J. I play low in tempo, but declarer lets the jack run then follows it with the ◇A and the ten. He overtakes that with the king as my partner pitches the ♡6, cashes two more diamonds, throwing clubs from the dummy, and then plays the ♡Q. My partner has thrown a second heart and the ♣J and, after winning with the king, I return a spade. Partner wins with the jack and cashes the ace, but declarer claims the rest.

This was the full deal:

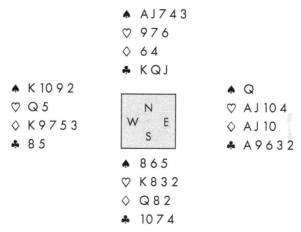

```
              ♠ A J 7 4 3
              ♡ 9 7 6
              ◇ 6 4
              ♣ K Q J
  ♠ K 10 9 2                    ♠ Q
  ♡ Q 5          N              ♡ A J 10 4
  ◇ K 9 7 5 3  W   E            ◇ A J 10
  ♣ 8 5          S              ♣ A 9 6 3 2
              ♠ 8 6 5
              ♡ K 8 3 2
              ◇ Q 8 2
              ♣ 10 7 4
```

POST-MORTEM

The winning defense should not have been difficult to find — I must cover the ◇J. That blocks the diamond suit, so after winning with the king and unblocking the diamonds, declarer can only try a heart towards the queen. I must go up with the king and return a spade; after winning with the jack partner switches to the ♣K, leaving declarer with only eight tricks.

In the other room the auction was identical save for the final double, and North led the ♣Q. If declarer wins this with dummy's ace and gets the diamonds right, he should always arrive at nine tricks, but he ducked. A spade switch puts the defenders one step ahead, but North went with the ♡7 and South won with the king and switched to a spade, North taking the ace and playing the ♣K. Declarer won, crossed to the ♡Q and played a diamond to the ten. South won and produced a club to defeat the contract.

When it comes to determining their moves, chess players can rely on those tried and tested by grandmasters in hundreds of games. Although bridge differs from chess in that the starting position is different on every deal, some situations can repeat themselves and it is useful to know the classics. On this deal from a knockout event, I pick up a modest hand as South:

Dealer North. ♠ K 6
N-S Vul. ♡ K 9 7 5 4
♢ Q 9 7
♣ 10 9 5

When my partner passes, East opens 1♣, promising 16+ points. When his partner makes a negative response of 1♢, he rebids 1♠ and repeats the suit over West's rebid of 2♣. That is enough for West to advance to game:

West	North	East	South
	pass	1♣*	pass
1♢*	pass	1♠	pass
2♣	pass	2♠	pass
4♠	all pass		

I can hope that my ♠K will be a trick, but where to find three more? Although I am not a fan of leading away from a king, circumstances alter cases and I start with the ♡5.

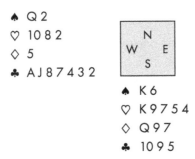

♠ Q 2
♡ 10 8 2
♢ 5
♣ A J 8 7 4 3 2

        ♠ K 6
        ♡ K 9 7 5 4
        ♢ Q 9 7
        ♣ 10 9 5

I am pleased to see partner produce the ace and he follows that with the queen, declarer playing the six and jack. At Trick 3 partner switches to the ♠3, but declarer wins with the ace, cashes the ♣K and the ◇A, ruffs a diamond, discards a heart on the ♣A and then ruffs a heart and gives up a trick to my ♠K.

This was the layout:

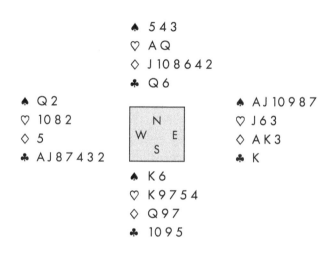

```
                    ♠ 5 4 3
                    ♡ A Q
                    ◇ J 10 8 6 4 2
                    ♣ Q 6
  ♠ Q 2                              ♠ A J 10 9 8 7
  ♡ 10 8 2          N                ♡ J 6 3
  ◇ 5           W       E            ◇ A K 3
  ♣ A J 8 7 4 3 2      S             ♣ K
                    ♠ K 6
                    ♡ K 9 7 5 4
                    ◇ Q 9 7
                    ♣ 10 9 5
```

POST-MORTEM

In the other room South led a diamond against 4♠, so declarer could win, unblock the ♣K, ruff a diamond, pitch a heart on the ♣A and take the spade finesse, finishing with ten tricks.

To defeat 4♠ I must overtake the ♡Q and give partner a ruff. Just in case you have not seen it before, here is the famous precedent from a match between the Dallas Aces and the Blue Team as described by Victor Mollo in Bridge Magazine:

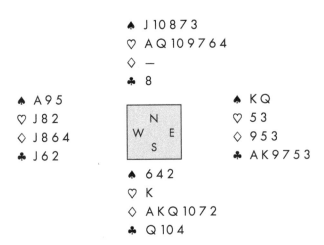

♠ J 10 8 7 3
♡ A Q 10 9 7 6 4
◊ —
♣ 8

♠ A 9 5
♡ J 8 2
◊ J 8 6 4
♣ J 6 2

N
W   E
S

♠ K Q
♡ 5 3
◊ 9 5 3
♣ A K 9 7 5 3

♠ 6 4 2
♡ K
◊ A K Q 10 7 2
♣ Q 10 4

In both rooms the contract was 4♡ by North, East-West remaining silent throughout the auction. The play to the first three tricks was the same. East led the ♣K, saw West's two, and switched to the ♠K. West encouraged with the ♠9 and the ♠Q took the next trick. Thereafter, in the Closed Room, Belladonna was in command, dummy's diamonds taking care of the three losing spades.

With the spades blocked, could the result be any different in the Open Room? Commentators and audience alike expected a flat board. Forquet took his time before playing to that third trick. Then, making up his mind, he overtook the ♠Q and gave Garozzo a ruff!

Forquet reasoned that, since Garozzo knew the club position after seeing the two, he would have cashed his ♣A had there been room for declarer to have another club. So, somehow, the defense had to take three tricks in spades, and it was significant that Garozzo, knowing that Forquet had the ♠A, led the ♠Q and not a low one. Maybe, of course, he had the ♠J too. But maybe he had started with a doubleton. It was a chance and Pietro Forquet was quick to seize it.

If I had reasoned this way I might have found the play of overtaking partner's ♡Q — and given us a shot at the IBPA's Defense of the Year award.

There is always debate as to the strongest pairs and individuals in the bridge world. In recent years, several players from the Low Countries have come to the fore. In an invitational teams event, the player on my right has a name that might loosely be interpreted as being connected with a vehicular occupation when I pick up these cards as South:

Dealer South.	♠ A K 9 7 3
E-W Vul.	♡ 4 2
	◇ J 10 8 3 2
	♣ 5

I have a gadget for this so I can open 2♠, promising a weak hand with spades and a minor suit. West has nothing to say, but when my partner raises to 3♠, East overcalls 4♡, ending the auction.

West	**North**	**East**	**South**
			2♠ *
pass	3♠	4♡	all pass

Recalling a dictum of the legendary Barry Crane, 'God dealt you the ace-king of a suit so you don't have a lead problem', I start with the ♠K, which in our methods asks partner to give count. These cards appear:

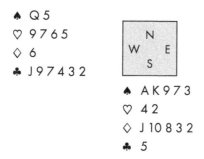

♠ Q 5
♡ 9 7 6 5
◇ 6
♣ J 9 7 4 3 2

N
W E
S

♠ A K 9 7 3
♡ 4 2
◇ J 10 8 3 2
♣ 5

Partner follows with the six and declarer the four. As partner would play the ♠6 from, say, ♠8642 or ♠J86, I can't be exactly sure how many spades he has. Given that we have two tricks in the spade suit, we need to find two more. If partner has the ♣A, I can switch to a club and a ruff will ensure at least one down. However, that might gift a finesse to declarer, who can only get to dummy via the trump suit, most likely by ruffing a diamond. There is also the possibility that declarer has the ◊AK, so if I switch to a club at Trick 2 he might be able to win and pitch a spade on a diamond.

Suppose I cash a second spade and exit with a diamond? If partner can win that and exit with a diamond, declarer can ruff and will then have to play trumps. In that situation, I can hope partner's club holding is too good for declarer, say ♣K108.

I decide to cash the ♠A; partner follows with the eight and declarer the two. I now know that declarer started with three spades. Suppose I switch to a club at this point? If declarer started with, say:

♠ 10 4 2   ♡ A Q J 10 8   ◊ K 9   ♣ A Q 8

then he will beat partner's card, ruff a spade and take the trump finesse. If he then reads me for a singleton club, he will cash the ♡A and eventually take a club finesse to get up to ten tricks. But if I play a diamond, partner can win and exit with a diamond or a spade; now declarer won't have enough entries to take all the finesses he needs.

Having made up my mind, I exit with the ◊J and partner wins with the ace and returns the ♡J. Declarer plays the queen and, when that wins, he ruffs the ◊9 and plays a second heart, taking partner's king with the ace. He then proceeds to ruff the ♠10 and play a club to the queen, claiming when it holds the trick.

The full deal:

```
                    ♠ J 8 6
                    ♡ K J
                    ◊ A Q 5 4
                    ♣ K 10 8 6
♠ Q 5                                    ♠ 10 4 2
♡ 9 7 6 5        ┌─────────┐            ♡ A Q 10 8 3
◊ 6              │    N    │            ◊ K 9 7
♣ J 9 7 4 3 2    │  W   E  │            ♣ A Q
                 │    S    │
                 └─────────┘
                    ♠ A K 9 7 3
                    ♡ 4 2
                    ◊ J 10 8 3 2
                    ♣ 5
```

POST-MORTEM

If I switch to my singleton club at Trick 3, partner covers dummy's card. Declarer wins and can ruff a spade and take the trump finesse, but there will only be nine tricks.

On balance, I'm inclined to think that switching to a club is a better bet.

At the other table, South also opened 2♠ but North passed. When East bid 3♡, West passed, but North bid 3♠ and West now came to life with 4♡. South cashed the ♠A and switched to a club; declarer won and exited with a spade. South took that and played a diamond, North winning and returning a club for South to ruff.

In the semifinal of a major knockout teams event I pick up these cards as South:

Dealer North.
Neither Vul.

♠ J 8 7 3
♡ A J 6 4
◇ K 3
♣ 9 7 5

When my partner can make no contribution, East opens 1♣ in the Polish style and West responds 1◇, which usually, but not always, promises 0-6. When East rebids 1NT to show a balanced hand with at least 18 points, West continues with 2♠, which shows a club suit and asks for range. When East shows a minimum with 2NT West bids 3♡, promising a good club suit and shortness in hearts, and East signs off in 3NT. This has been the complex auction:

West	North	East	South
	pass	1♣*	pass
1◇*	pass	1NT*	pass
2♠*	pass	2NT*	pass
3♡*	pass	3NT	all pass

Knowing that dummy is short in hearts I lead a fourth-best ♡4:

♠ 10 4 2
♡ 9
◇ J 2
♣ A J 10 6 4 3 2

```
      N
  W       E
      S
```

♠ J 8 7 3
♡ A J 6 4
◇ K 3
♣ 9 7 5

Partner covers dummy's nine with the ten; declarer wins with the king and runs the ♣Q, partner winning with the king. He returns the ♡3, covered by the eight and my jack as a spade goes from dummy. With six tricks in view in dummy, it is clear that this is the critical moment for the defense.

I know declarer has the ♡Q (partner would have played it at Trick 1) but where is the ♡2? If my partner has it (having started with ♡107532), declarer's queen will now fall under my ace. If declarer has it, then I need to find partner's entry. In terms of high cards, I know declarer started with the ♡KQ and the ♣Q. That leaves 11-12 points in spades and diamonds. Declarer could have the ♠AKQ and the ◇Q, the ♠AQ and the ◇AQ, or the ♠KQ and the ◇AQ. Eventually I decide to give myself two chances. I lay down the ♡A but it is declarer who produces the two. Hoping that partner has the other red ace, I switch to the ◇K, but declarer is able to face his cards when this proves to be the layout:

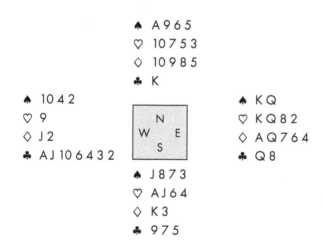

	♠ A 9 6 5	
	♡ 10 7 5 3	
	◇ 10 9 8 5	
	♣ K	
♠ 10 4 2		♠ K Q
♡ 9		♡ K Q 8 2
◇ J 2		◇ A Q 7 6 4
♣ A J 10 6 4 3 2		♣ Q 8
	♠ J 8 7 3	
	♡ A J 6 4	
	◇ K 3	
	♣ 9 7 5	

Our partnership plays that, after a strong club and a negative response, a double promises the majors and 1NT the minors, but a Polish 1♣ does not have to be based on a strong hand, so that does not help South here.

Conventional wisdom is that North should return his fourth-best heart in this situation but as it happens the ♡7 works well, as South will then think North has only three hearts and try to find North's entry for another heart play. The trouble with doing this is that South might have started with five hearts and guess to put North in with a diamond rather than a spade.

In the other room, East opened 1♢ and raised West's 1NT response to game. North led the ♡5 to the king and ace and South returned a heart to the ten and queen. When North came in with the ♣K he carefully cashed the ♠A before playing a third heart.

Having examined my conscience in the matter, I cannot say that my defense was wrong.

Richard Tauber became the most popular singer in Austria and Germany during the 1930s. One of his greatest hits was Dein ist Mein Ganzes Herz –– You are my heart's delight. On this deal from a mixed event, the player on my right is a multiple world champion noted for her amusing repartee. One of her favorite sayings is, 'No money, no honey'. These are my cards in the South seat:

Dealer South.	♠ A Q 8 6
Both Vul.	♡ J 6 2
	◊ 5
	♣ Q 7 5 3 2

After three passes, East opens 1♡ and jumps to 4♡ over her partner's 1NT response, giving this brief sequence:

West	North	East	South
			pass
pass	pass	1♡	pass
1NT	pass	4♡	all pass

I lead my diamond and dummy has a couple of useful cards:

♠ 9 7 2
♡ K 9
◊ A 8 6 4 3 2
♣ 9 4

```
        N
   W         E
        S
```

♠ A Q 8 6
♡ J 6 2
◊ 5
♣ Q 7 5 3 2

Declarer plays low from dummy, my partner winning the trick with the king and returning the ◊7, declarer following with the nine and queen. I ruff and switch to the three of clubs, but declarer takes partner's king with the ace and plays the ♡3. When I follow with the six she plays dummy's ♡9 and, after it holds, she ruffs a diamond high, returns to dummy with the ♡K and discards her losers on the established diamonds, making eleven tricks.

This was the full deal:

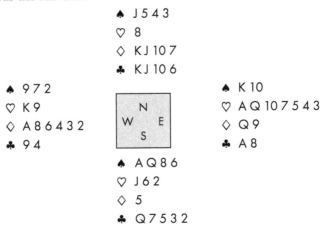

```
                    ♠ J 5 4 3
                    ♡ 8
                    ◇ K J 10 7
                    ♣ K J 10 6
  ♠ 9 7 2                              ♠ K 10
  ♡ K 9              N                 ♡ A Q 10 7 5 4 3
  ◇ A 8 6 4 3 2    W   E               ◇ Q 9
  ♣ 9 4              S                 ♣ A 8
                    ♠ A Q 8 6
                    ♡ J 6 2
                    ◇ 5
                    ♣ Q 7 5 3 2
```

POST-MORTEM

Assuming declarer held only two diamonds, it should have been possible to work out that there was nothing to be gained by ruffing the second diamond. If South discards, declarer cannot come to more than nine tricks.

UPPERCUT

An uppercut can be an effective weapon in boxing, and the term has been adopted by bridge, in which it indicates a defensive play where one of the defenders ruffs high, thereby promoting a trump trick for partner. During the Open Pairs at the European Open Championships, I hold these cards as South:

Dealer West.	♠	A K 10
E-W Vul.	♡	8 5
	◇	Q 6 2
	♣	10 8 7 6 2

When West opens 1♡ my partner overcalls 1♠ and East bids 4◇, promising a shortage in diamonds and good heart support. Tempted by my excellent trumps I decide to sacrifice with 4♠ and, somewhat to my relief, West continues with 5♡, leaving us with this auction:

West	North	East	South
1♡	1♠	4◇*	4♠
5♡	all pass		

My partner leads the ♠Q and dummy is substantial:

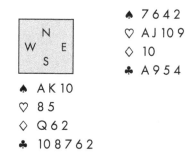

```
                        ♠ 7 6 4 2
             N          ♡ A J 10 9
        W         E     ◇ 10
             S          ♣ A 9 5 4
        ♠ A K 10
        ♡ 8 5
        ◇ Q 6 2
        ♣ 10 8 7 6 2
```

I overtake the ♠Q with the king, and when declarer follows with the five I switch to the ♣6, covered by the queen, king and ace. Declarer now plays dummy's ♣4, partner winning with the jack and exiting with a spade. Declarer ruffs this and embarks on a crossruff, reaching this position:

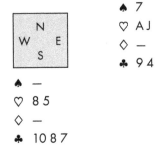

```
                        ♠  7
                        ♡  A J
                        ◇  —
                        ♣  9 4
          N
       W     E
          S

    ♠  —
    ♡  8 5
    ◇  —
    ♣  10 8 7
```

When he plays dummy's last spade, I discard a club, and he then shows his cards, claiming the rest on a high crossruff.

This was the layout:

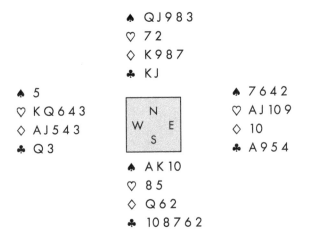

```
                    ♠  Q J 9 8 3
                    ♡  7 2
                    ◇  K 9 8 7
                    ♣  K J

    ♠  5                             ♠  7 6 4 2
    ♡  K Q 6 4 3                     ♡  A J 10 9
    ◇  A J 5 4 3        N            ◇  10
    ♣  Q 3          W       E        ♣  A 9 5 4
                        S
                    ♠  A K 10
                    ♡  8 5
                    ◇  Q 6 2
                    ♣  10 8 7 6 2
```

POST-MORTEM

On this deal, who would believe that the ♡7 could have won a trick for the defense? After all, declarer held ♡AKQJ109643 between the two hands, so surely you cannot lose a trick to the seven.

This was the position when declarer played dummy's last spade:

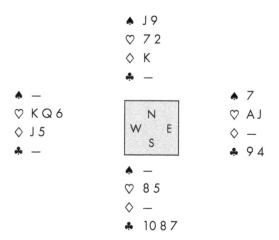

```
                ♠ J 9
                ♡ 7 2
                ◇ K
                ♣ —
  ♠ —                          ♠ 7
  ♡ K Q 6        N             ♡ A J
  ◇ J 5      W       E         ◇ —
  ♣ —            S             ♣ 9 4
                ♠ —
                ♡ 8 5
                ◇ —
                ♣ 10 8 7
```

If South ruffs with the ♡8, declarer has to overruff, but if he then ruffs a diamond, cashes a heart and plays a club, North's ♡7 comes into its own.

At first sight it may appear that an initial trump lead defeats 5♡, but that is not the case. Declarer wins in dummy, cashes the ◇A, ruffs a diamond and gives up a spade. Say South wins and plays a second trump. Declarer wins, ruffs a diamond, ruffs a spade and plays a diamond. North wins, but unable to play a club must exit with a spade. Declarer ruffs and cashes his red winners, squeezing North in the black suits.

They would have murdered us in 4♠ doubled.

During the qualifying rounds of a long pairs event, I pick up these miserable cards sitting South against formidable opposition:

Dealer South.　　♠ 10 4 3
Both Vul.　　　　♡ Q 3
　　　　　　　　　♢ J 10 7 6 4
　　　　　　　　　♣ J 9 4

There are days on which I would consider opening my hand with a weak 2♢, but here both the vulnerability and our system are against me. When West opens 1♢ it signifies a limited (11-15) hand that might only contain one diamond. When my partner makes a takeout double, East bids 1♡, which is a transfer to spades. West's rebid of 2♣ sees East jump to 3♠, and West's 3NT concludes this auction:

West	North	East	South
			pass
1♢*	dbl	1♡*	pass
2♣	pass	3♠	pass
3NT	all pass		

My partner leads a fourth-best ♡2:

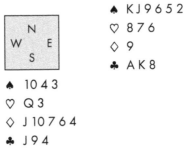

♠ K J 9 6 5 2
♡ 8 7 6
♢ 9
♣ A K 8

♠ 10 4 3
♡ Q 3
♢ J 10 7 6 4
♣ J 9 4

When I play the queen, declarer wins with the king and plays the ♣5 to dummy's king, partner following with the two. His next move is to play the ♢9, and when I cover with the ten, that is followed by the queen and ace. My partner continues with the ♡4 and declarer wins with the nine and plays two rounds of clubs, partner winning with the queen and exiting with a third heart. Declarer wins this with the ♡A, cashes the ♡J, partner pitching the ♠7, and with these cards remaining, he plays the master club:

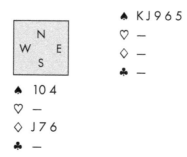

		♠ K J 9 6 5
		♡ —
		◇ —
		♣ —

♠ 10 4
♡ —
◇ J 7 6
♣ —

From the bidding and play so far it seems clear declarer started with a 0=4=5=4 shape. If I throw a diamond, he will cash the ◇K and exit with a diamond, and dummy will be certain of taking a trick with the ♠K. To avoid this, I discard the ♠4. Declarer continues with the ◇3, and when partner follows with the ◇2, I win and exit with the ♠10. Declarer discards a diamond and when partner follows with the ♠8, declarer calls for dummy's nine! Left on play, I have to lead into declarer's ◇K8.

This was the layout:

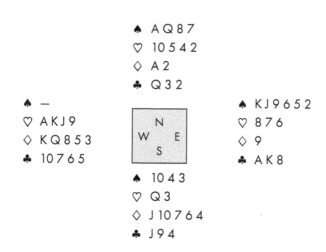

```
              ♠ A Q 8 7
              ♡ 10 5 4 2
              ◇ A 2
              ♣ Q 3 2

♠ —                            ♠ K J 9 6 5 2
♡ A K J 9         N            ♡ 8 7 6
◇ K Q 8 5 3    W     E         ◇ 9
♣ 10 7 6 5        S            ♣ A K 8

              ♠ 10 4 3
              ♡ Q 3
              ◇ J 10 7 6 4
              ♣ J 9 4
```

When declarer cashed the last club, this was the position:

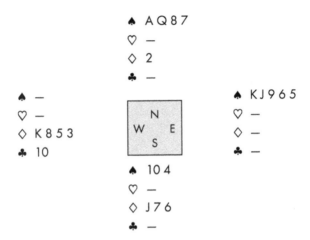

It is right to throw a spade, but it should be the ten! Then declarer cannot duck the spade exit and North will take the last two tricks with the ♠AQ.

At the point where partner won the ◇A, the only winning defense is for him to exit with the ♣3 — clearly impossible to find. Having been gifted a fourth heart trick (partner was hoping I held the ♡9), declarer could have cashed his winners in that suit before playing clubs, which would have left the defenders helpless.

Distant Memory

Although contract bridge has been around for almost 100 years, there is still no consensus as to the best bidding system. After starting out with Acol, I became enamored of strong club systems such as Blue Club and Precision. I have been dragged out of retirement by an old friend, and we are attempting to recapture some our lost youth by adopting a complex version of the latter, when I pick up these cards as South during the qualifying rounds of the Reisinger Cup:

Dealer South. ♠ —
N-S Vul.   ♡ Q 9 4 2
               ◇ K J 7 5 3
               ♣ K Q 7 2

I open 1◇, which under certain circumstances might be based on a void. When West overcalls 1♠ my partner has nothing to say, and East draws matters to a close by jumping to 3NT:

West	North	East	South
			1◇*
1♠	pass	3NT	all pass

Players who jump to game in this situation tend to have a decent holding in the opening bidder's suit, so I think my choice lies between a club and a heart. I have some vague recollection of reading about which card is best to lead if I choose a club, but eventually I opt for the ♡2 to reveal this dummy:

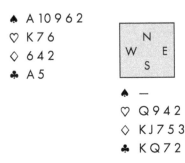

♠ A 10 9 6 2
♡ K 7 6
◇ 6 4 2
♣ A 5

♠ —
♡ Q 9 4 2
◇ K J 7 5 3
♣ K Q 7 2

Partner can only produce the five, and declarer wins with the eight and promptly returns the jack. When I withhold the queen, partner following with the three, declarer continues with a heart to dummy's king, on which partner discards the ◇10. Now declarer crosses to hand with a spade to the king, partner following with the three as I discard the ◇3. That makes declarer pause for thought. Eventually he cashes the ♡A, pitching a spade from dummy, which is matched by partner's ♠4. His next move is a club to dummy's ace followed by a low club, partner following with the jack and nine. I overtake the nine, cash the queen and exit with the ♣7, partner winning with the ten and returning the ◇9. However, declarer wins with the ace and plays a spade to the nine to endplay my partner.

The full deal:

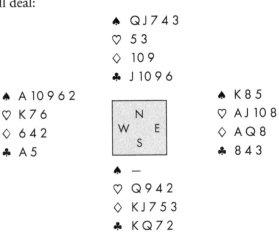

♠ Q J 7 4 3
♡ 5 3
◇ 10 9
♣ J 10 9 6

♠ A 10 9 6 2
♡ K 7 6
◇ 6 4 2
♣ A 5

♠ K 8 5
♡ A J 10 8
◇ A Q 8
♣ 8 4 3

♠ —
♡ Q 9 4 2
◇ K J 7 5 3
♣ K Q 7 2

It would not have helped if North had returned the ♠Q — declarer wins in dummy, plays a diamond to the ace and exits with a spade, forcing North to surrender the last trick to dummy.

I could have ensured the demise of the contract by splitting my club honors on the first round of the suit. Declarer wins and exits with a club but now we can defeat the contract several times over. One way is for North to switch to a diamond — I win and we now cash two clubs, after which North has a safe exit in spades.

Eventually a memory stirred about the club suit — Winning Notrump Leads by David Bird and Taf Anthias makes it clear that leading an honor is best from this type of combination — and it would have simplified the defense on this deal, although it does not guarantee the defeat of the contract. Declarer ducks, wins the next club and plays a spade to the eight followed by the ♡J. If South ducks this and then covers the next heart, declarer wins in dummy, plays a spade to the king and exits with a club. If South wins and exits with a club, North can win and switch to a diamond but declarer goes up with the ace and plays a spade to the ace, strip-squeezing South.

As the play went, if declarer had put in the ♠8 on the first round of the suit he would have been on course for an overtrick!

In the other room they also started with a Precision 1◇ and West overcalled 1♠. East cuebid 2◇ and then passed West's 2♠ rebid. Declarer won the club lead, cashed the ♠A and played a spade to the jack and king. His next move was to run the ♡J, which meant he was sure of eight tricks, and if he plays a spade at this point he should come to nine. In practice he continued with the ♡10 to the queen and king; when he played a third heart North ruffed and played a diamond, restricting declarer to +110.

Bridge was affected in exactly the same way as other sporting activities by the Covid-19 virus that swept the world in 2020. The World and European Championships were postponed and countless other events fell by the wayside. However, eventually life returned to normal and tournaments enjoyed an upsurge in entries, especially those in exotic locations. On a sun-drenched island in the North Atlantic, I pick up this modest collection in the South seat:

```
Dealer North.       ♠ Q764
N-S Vul.            ♡ A743
                    ◇ J82
                    ♣ 96
```

My partner opens 2◇, the multicolored version, denoting a weak hand in one of the majors. When East overcalls 2♠, I know my partner's suit, but given the vulnerability there is little point in advertising the fact. If anything, it may only serve to help the opponents. When I pass, West leaps to 6♠, giving us this auction:

West	North	East	South
	2◇*	2♠	pass
6♠	all pass		

I lead the ♡A and dummy looks threatening:

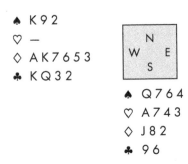

```
♠ K92
♡ —
◇ AK7653
♣ KQ32

              N
            W   E
              S

          ♠ Q764
          ♡ A743
          ◇ J82
          ♣ 96
```

Declarer ruffs in dummy (partner encourages with the ♡9) and calls for the ♠9, partner following with the five. I win with the queen and play a second heart, but declarer ruffs, plays three rounds of diamonds, ruffing the third one with the ♠8, draws trumps and claims. This was the full deal:

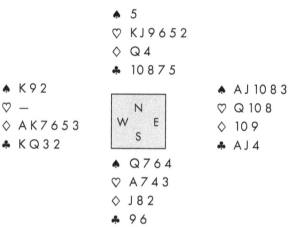

```
                    ♠ 5
                    ♡ KJ9652
                    ◇ Q4
                    ♣ 10875

♠ K92                               ♠ AJ1083
♡ —             N                   ♡ Q108
◇ AK7653     W     E                ◇ 109
♣ KQ32          S                   ♣ AJ4

                    ♠ Q764
                    ♡ A743
                    ◇ J82
                    ♣ 96
```

POST-MORTEM

There was no rush to take the ♠Q. If South ducks, declarer cannot get up to twelve tricks. Cashing the ♠K leaves declarer with no way to dispose of his hearts in time, while if he plays three rounds of diamonds, ruffs a heart and then throws a heart on a winning diamond, South ruffs and exits with a heart, securing a second trick with the ♠Q.

42   THE PIN IS MIGHTIER
THAN THE SWORD

Every four years the World Bridge Series affords everyone the opportunity to compete for a world title. Having made a long trip to the home of Mickey Mouse, I find myself looking at these cards as South:

Dealer South.
Neither Vul.

♠ A 10 8 4
♡ Q 5 2
◇ J 8 2
♣ K Q 9

I open 1♣, which in our methods could be based on as few as two clubs. When West overcalls 1♡ my partner jumps to 5♣, marking him with a significant number of clubs. East has nothing to say, but West is not finished and he continues with a double, which sees East bid 5♠. This is how the auction unfolded:

West	North	East	South
			1♣*
1♡	5♣	pass	pass
dbl	pass	5♠	all pass

I lead the ♣K and dummy is well endowed:

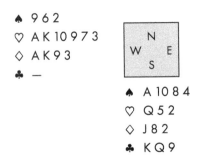

♠ 9 6 2
♡ A K 10 9 7 3
◇ A K 9 3
♣ —

♠ A 10 8 4
♡ Q 5 2
◇ J 8 2
♣ K Q 9

Declarer ruffs and plays a spade to the king, partner following with the ♠3. I duck in tempo and declarer tables the ♡6. When I play the two, he lets the six run and it holds the trick, partner contributing the four. Now declarer ruffs a club and plays three rounds of hearts, pitching a club. I ruff and exit with a diamond, but declarer wins in dummy, cashes another diamond, ruffs a diamond and plays the ♠Q, claiming his contract.

The full deal:

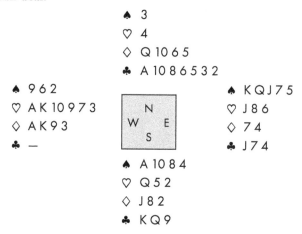

	♠ 3	
	♡ 4	
	◇ Q 10 6 5	
	♣ A 10 8 6 5 3 2	
♠ 9 6 2		♠ K Q J 7 5
♡ A K 10 9 7 3		♡ J 8 6
◇ A K 9 3		◇ 7 4
♣ —		♣ J 7 4
	♠ A 10 8 4	
	♡ Q 5 2	
	◇ J 8 2	
	♣ K Q 9	

POST-MORTEM

The winning defense is for South to take the first spade and return the ♠10, pinning dummy's nine. Then the best declarer can do is to win, cash another spade and run the ♡6. Eventually South will ruff a heart and cash a club for one down.

Later on it occurred to me that declarer's play could have been improved upon. Suppose South is 4=3=2=4 — were that to be the distribution declarer's line would fail, as after ruffing the fourth heart South exits with a diamond locking declarer in dummy and ensuring a trump promotion. Declarer can avoid this grisly outcome by cashing dummy's top diamonds before taking a discard on the hearts — a perfect example of the so-called Dentist's Coup.

While the COVID-19 virus ran its course, bridge players survived in a variety of ways. As events were postponed or canceled, special tournaments were organized on the Internet thanks to the cooperation of sites such as Bridge Base and Bid72. During one of these, I am dealt as South:

Dealer North.   ♠ A Q 10 9 6
Neither Vul.   ♡ K 6 2
                 ◊ 6
                 ♣ 10 9 4 3

When my partner passes, East opens 1♡ and I overcall 1♠. West has nothing to say but my partner jumps to 3♡, which we play as a mixed raise promising four-card spade support. East is not finished, and when he doubles I content myself with 3♠. Like a housefly one cannot seem to get rid of, East doubles for a second time and West's 4♡ leaves us with this auction:

West	North	East	South
	pass	1♡	1♠
pass	3♡*	dbl	3♠
pass	pass	dbl	pass
4♡	all pass		

Naturally, I lead my singleton diamond and dummy is not immediately terrifying:

♠ J 5 2
♡ Q 5
◊ 10 8 4 2
♣ Q J 6 2

```
        N
    W       E
        S
```

♠ A Q 10 9 6
♡ K 6 2
◊ 6
♣ 10 9 4 3

When declarer calls for dummy's two, partner plays the seven. Declarer wins with the queen, cashes the ♣A, partner following with the five, and then plays the ♠7. I would like partner to win this trick so I play the ♠6. When dummy plays the jack, partner wins with the king and returns the ◇K, which I ruff after declarer covers with the ace. These cards remain:

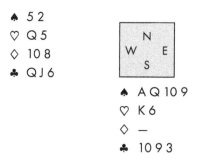

                    ♠ 5 2
                    ♡ Q 5
                    ◇ 10 8
                    ♣ Q J 6

                              N
                          W   E
                              S

                    ♠ A Q 10 9
                    ♡ K 6
                    ◇ —
                    ♣ 10 9 3

We have taken two tricks and my ♡K will be a third — where to find a fourth? I think my best chance must be to hope partner has three hearts, so I exit with the ♠A. Declarer ruffs, cashes the ♣K and continues with the ♡4. I take my king and exit with another spade, but declarer ruffs, plays a heart to dummy's queen and then discards two diamonds on dummy's clubs.

This was the full deal:

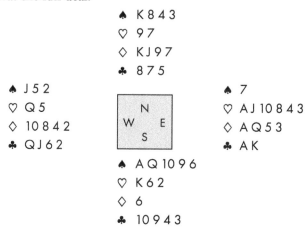

                    ♠ K 8 4 3
                    ♡ 9 7
                    ◇ K J 9 7
                    ♣ 8 7 5

    ♠ J 5 2   ♠ 7
    ♡ Q 5   N   ♡ A J 10 8 4 3
    ◇ 10 8 4 2   W   E   ◇ A Q 5 3
    ♣ Q J 6 2   S   ♣ A K

                    ♠ A Q 10 9 6
                    ♡ K 6 2
                    ◇ 6
                    ♣ 10 9 4 3

This was the situation after South had ruffed the ◇A:

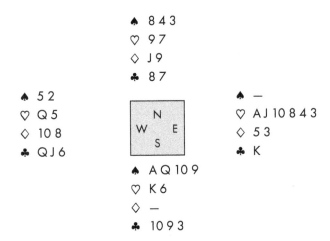

```
              ♠ 8 4 3
              ♡ 9 7
              ◇ J 9
              ♣ 8 7
♠ 5 2                        ♠ —
♡ Q 5           N           ♡ A J 10 8 4 3
◇ 10 8      W       E       ◇ 5 3
♣ Q J 6         S           ♣ K
              ♠ A Q 10 9
              ♡ K 6
              ◇ —
              ♣ 10 9 3
```

To defeat the contract, South must return the ♡6! Although this gives up the natural trump trick, it ensures that declarer cannot reach dummy's winning clubs and will therefore lose two diamonds.

Although it was tempting to lead the singleton, if South starts with a trump, declarer will have no real chance.

In the other room, South also led his diamond, but after winning with the queen, declarer unblocked the clubs and then played a low heart. South went in with the king and underled his spades to North's king; he scored a diamond ruff, but declarer could reach dummy with the ♡Q and discard his losing diamonds.

Frozen

Bridge is awash with terms describing all manner of things. One of my favorites is the 'frozen suit'. I recall Patrick Jourdain using the term many years ago, but it is unclear who invented it (not, as Ron Tacchi suggests, Captain Birdseye). In a post on his excellent web site around the beginning of April 2020, Richard Pavlicek announced that 'PavCo attorneys today filed a class-action suit against Walt Disney Studios for its unlawful appropriation of a bridge term for an animated film. Financial recovery is expected to exceed $500 million, and qualified claimants must register by April 30, midnight GMT. To be eligible you must be a member in good standing of a national bridge organization, or a homeless derelict; we don't really care. The key is to be alive, which puts us one up on Disney'.

During the Rosenblum round of 32 I pick up these cards as South:

Dealer South.	♠ K 10 2
E-W Vul.	♡ A 10 6 4
	♢ J 2
	♣ A 10 8 6

When I open 1♣, my partner responds 1♡ and I raise to 2♡. West now enters from the wings with a double, presumably showing spades and diamonds, and my partner redoubles, suggesting he has a decent hand and some interest in playing for a penalty. When East bids 2♠ I decide to double, which ends the auction:

West	North	East	South
			1♣
pass	1♡	pass	2♡
dbl	redbl	2♠	dbl
all pass			

When you hold the balance of power it can be a good idea to lead a trump, but my ♠10 might be important. Expecting partner to have some diamond values, I start with the ◇J:

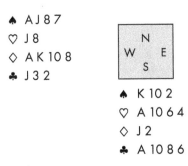

♠ A J 8 7
♡ J 8
◇ A K 10 8
♣ J 3 2

♠ K 10 2
♡ A 10 6 4
◇ J 2
♣ A 10 8 6

So much for partner's hypothetical diamond values!

Declarer wins with dummy's ace, playing the five from his hand as partner follows with the three, and continues with the ♡J. Partner follows with the nine and I win with the ace and play a second diamond to dummy's king, partner following with the seven and declarer the six. Partner wins the heart continuation with the queen and plays the ◇Q, on which I discard the ♡6 as declarer follows with the nine. Partner's next card is the ♣4, which promises an honor in the suit. When declarer plays the nine, I win with the ace and return the ten. Declarer wins that with the king and plays a spade to dummy's seven. Partner wins with the queen and plays the ♣Q, but declarer ruffs and plays a spade to the jack, claiming the rest when partner follows.

The full deal:

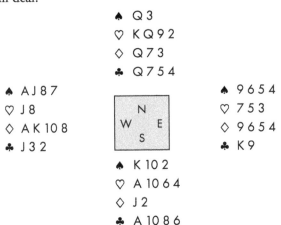

```
              ♠ Q 3
              ♡ K Q 9 2
              ◇ Q 7 3
              ♣ Q 7 5 4
♠ A J 8 7                        ♠ 9 6 5 4
♡ J 8            N              ♡ 7 5 3
◇ A K 10 8    W     E           ◇ 9 6 5 4
♣ J 3 2          S              ♣ K 9
              ♠ K 10 2
              ♡ A 10 6 4
              ◇ J 2
              ♣ A 10 8 6
```

South's mistake was to play the ♣A. If he puts in the ten, declarer wins with the jack and returns a club, but South can now win and play a third club. Declarer ruffs and plays a spade to the seven, but North wins and exits with a heart; South must score another trump for one down.

A simpler defense is for North to exit with a heart rather than a club, leaving declarer to tackle the frozen suit.

In the replay, the bidding was identical, save for the final double. South led the ♣8 — a reasonable shot, but as it turned out the only suit to give declarer a chance at the contract. Declarer took North's queen with the king and played a spade to the seven and queen. North switched to the ♡Q, followed by the king, which South overtook with the ace to continue with the ten. Declarer ruffed in dummy and exited with a club, South winning with the ten and playing the ace, which declarer ruffed. A spade went to the ten and jack and now all declarer had to do was play three rounds of diamonds. North would win, but would then have no good move.

Missing this, declarer drew the outstanding trump, and when he played for the diamonds to be 4-1 he went two down.

Anyone who watches the major golf championships will have noticed that because of the punishing rough several players sometimes make use of something termed a 'rescue club' to get them out of an awkward situation. During the semifinals of a Mixed Teams event I pick up these cards as South:

Dealer East.   ♠ A J 2
N-S Vul.   ♡ K 8 7 6 4 2
              ◇ 9 8
              ♣ 9 5

When East opens 1♠, I consider overcalling 2♡, but although I have a six-card suit my intermediates are poor and I decide to pass. West raises to 2♠ and that travels back to me. Although I was not disposed to overcall at the two-level, I now know the opponents have a fit and partner is marked with a spade shortage. In this type of situation, it is invariably correct to balance and I bid 3♡. When West goes on to 3♠, it leaves us with this sequence:

West	North	East	South
		1♠	pass
2♠	pass	pass	3♡
3♠	all pass		

In general terms I consider leading away from a king to be a losing policy, but as it is likely that partner will have an honor in the suit I start with the ♡6:

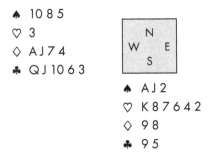

♠ 10 8 5
♡ 3
◇ A J 7 4
♣ Q J 10 6 3

         ♠ A J 2
         ♡ K 8 7 6 4 2
         ◇ 9 8
         ♣ 9 5

When partner plays the ♡10, declarer wins with the queen, ruffs the ♡9 in dummy and plays the ♠10 to the four, the three and my jack. Needing to find some tricks I switch to the ♣9, hoping to find partner with ♣AKx. When declarer plays dummy's queen and partner follows with the eight that proves to be a forlorn hope, and declarer continues with the ♠8. Partner produces the king and switches to the ◇3, but declarer plays the queen and faces her cards, conceding only the two missing aces.

This was the layout:

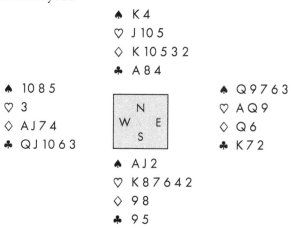

```
              ♠ K 4
              ♡ J 10 5
              ◇ K 10 5 3 2
              ♣ A 8 4
   ♠ 10 8 5                      ♠ Q 9 7 6 3
   ♡ 3              N            ♡ A Q 9
   ◇ A J 7 4     W     E         ◇ Q 6
   ♣ Q J 10 6 3     S            ♣ K 7 2
              ♠ A J 2
              ♡ K 8 7 6 4 2
              ◇ 9 8
              ♣ 9 5
```

POST-MORTEM

Despite the unfortunate choice of opening lead, it was still possible to defeat the contract in more than one way. Simplest would have been for South to switch to a diamond when in with the ♠J. Having missed that, the answer is for South to overtake the ♠K with the ace and switch to a diamond. Declarer has to finesse and North wins with the king, cashes the ♣A and plays her remaining club, resurrecting the ♠2.

In the other room South did not compete and found the excellent lead of the ◇9 against 2♠, North winning with the king. If North switches to a heart at this point even 2♠ can be defeated, but that is hardly obvious and North returned the ◇2, declarer winning with the queen. Best now is to go after the side suit, but declarer cashed the ♡A, ruffed a heart and ran the ♠10. South won and can now play a club, North taking the ace, cashing the ♠K and then playing a heart. Again, this is hard to see and South opted to return a heart, declarer ruffing in dummy and playing a club. North took the ace, but now declarer was in control and lost only the top trumps for +110.

It is easy to lose concentration when holding a poor hand — one tends to assume that partner will be the one with the decisions to make. However, that is not always the case. On this deal from a Swiss Teams event, my partner is a top-ranking expert, while our opponents are unknown. In the middle of the match I pick up a hand as South that reminds me of a typical night at the rubber-bridge table:

Dealer South.
E-W Vul.

♠ 10 3
♡ 10 8 4
♢ 9 8 7 5 2
♣ 8 6 3

Although age has not diminished my imagination, I resist the temptation to open the bidding. When West opens 1♣, East responds 1♠ and after West jumps to 4♠, East asks for keycards. When West shows two without the ♠Q, East bids 6NT to leave this auction:

West	North	East	South
			pass
1♣	pass	1♠	pass
4♠	pass	4NT*	pass
5♡*	pass	6NT	all pass

With nothing to go on I lead the ♢8, and dummy is roughly what one might expect for a jump to 4♠:

♠ 7 6 4 2
♡ K J 9 7
♢ A
♣ A K Q 9

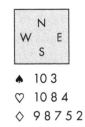

♠ 10 3
♡ 10 8 4
♢ 9 8 7 5 2
♣ 8 6 3

When declarer wins with dummy's ace, partner follows with the four and declarer the six. His next move is to play the ♠2, which goes to the eight, nine and my ten. That's unexpected! Not wanting to give anything away I return the ♣6 and declarer wins in hand with the jack, cashes the ♡AQ and ◇K, and returns to dummy with a club to play winners. In the three-card ending declarer plays dummy's ♣Q and partner folds his cards.

This was the full deal:

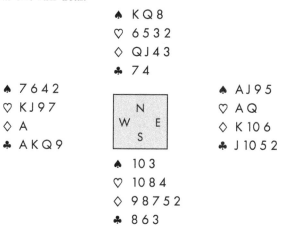

```
              ♠ K Q 8
              ♡ 6 5 3 2
              ◇ Q J 4 3
              ♣ 7 4
♠ 7 6 4 2              ♠ A J 9 5
♡ K J 9 7      N       ♡ A Q
◇ A        W     E     ◇ K 10 6
♣ A K Q 9      S       ♣ J 10 5 2
              ♠ 10 3
              ♡ 10 8 4
              ◇ 9 8 7 5 2
              ♣ 8 6 3
```

POST-MORTEM

This was the position at the end:

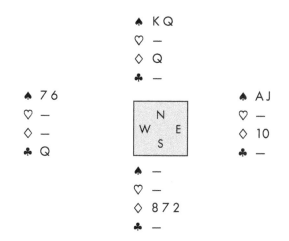

```
              ♠ K Q
              ♡ —
              ◇ Q
              ♣ —
♠ 7 6                 ♠ A J
♡ —        N          ♡ —
◇ —    W     E        ◇ 10
♣ Q        S          ♣ —
              ♠ —
              ♡ —
              ◇ 8 7 2
              ♣ —
```

When declarer cashed the ♣Q, North had no answer.

Counter-intuitively, having won a trick with the ♠10, South must return a spade, removing the entry to declarer's hand and breaking up the impending squeeze. Once you put your mind to it, you can see that this play cannot cost.

At the other table, West splintered with 4◇ over 1♠ and North doubled, which induced South to bid 5◇ over East's subsequent 4NT. That would have gone for 1700, but East preferred to play in 5♠.

As to the bidding at my table, it occurred to me that East might have bid 6♣ over 5♡, offering West a choice of contracts. With such poor spades, it will not be difficult for West to do the right thing.

THE LONG VIEW

Once popular, multiple team events are now almost non-existent, having given way to events using the Swiss pairing system. However, my club clings to tradition and stages one every month. Playing against one of the weaker teams, I pick up this modest collection in the South chair:

Dealer West. ♠ 10 6
E-W Vul. ♡ J 10 9 7
  ◇ K 3 2
  ♣ Q J 9 6

West and partner have nothing to say, but East opens 2♣ and rebids a Kokish 2♡ over West's response of 2◇. That is a relay, promising either hearts or a very strong balanced hand. When West obediently bids 2♠, East's 3♣ indicates he has hearts and clubs. West continues with 3♡, and East's advance to 4♡ leaves us with this sequence:

West	North	East	South
pass	pass	2♣ *	pass
2◇*	pass	2♡*	pass
2♠*	pass	3♣	pass
3♡	pass	4♡	all pass

With my potentially excellent holding in both of declarer's suits I look no further that the ♡J for my opening lead:

♠ K 9 7 4 2
♡ Q 3
◇ J 9 5
♣ 10 8 7

  ♠ 10 6
  ♡ J 10 9 7
  ◇ K 3 2
  ♣ Q J 9 6

Declarer plays low from dummy and wins with the ace, partner following with the five. He continues with the ♠J, and when that holds he plays the ♠Q. Partner wins with the ace and returns the ♡8, which runs to dummy's queen. When declarer plays dummy's ♠K and pitches the ◇6 from his hand, I ruff and exit with my last trump. Declarer wins and proceeds to cash two more trumps. This is the position as the last of these hits the table:

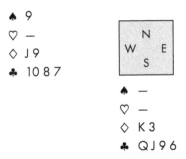

```
    ♠ 9
    ♡ —
    ◇ J 9
    ♣ 10 8 7
    
    ♠ —
    ♡ —
    ◇ K 3
    ♣ Q J 9 6
```

When I discard the ◇3, declarer lays down the ◇A and then exits with the ♣2. I win with the jack and continue with the queen, but declarer wins, plays a club to dummy's ten and scores the game-going trick with the ♠9.

This was the full layout:

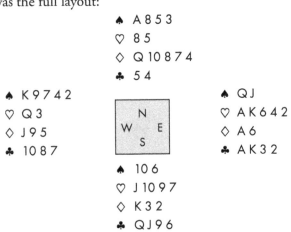

```
              ♠ A 8 5 3
              ♡ 8 5
              ◇ Q 10 8 7 4
              ♣ 5 4
♠ K 9 7 4 2                    ♠ Q J
♡ Q 3                         ♡ A K 6 4 2
◇ J 9 5                       ◇ A 6
♣ 10 8 7                      ♣ A K 3 2
              ♠ 10 6
              ♡ J 10 9 7
              ◇ K 3 2
              ♣ Q J 9 6
```

Having ruffed the ♠K, South must exit with a diamond. That should not have been a difficult play to find, as declarer was marked with a 2=5=2=4 pattern.

In the replay, East started with a Precision club and when West responded 1◊, North bid 2◊, doubled by East and raised to 3◊ by South. After West ended the bidding with a jump to 4♠, North led the ◊7. South won with the king and returned the three, declarer winning with dummy's ace and playing the ♠J. When that held, he continued with the ♠Q and North ducked for a second time. It made no difference, declarer playing three rounds of hearts to dispose of his remaining diamond. North could ruff and play a club, but declarer won in dummy and ruffed a heart, establishing the ♡6 for the discard of the losing club.

In a high-stakes rubber-bridge game, my partner's nickname is 'The Tate Gallery', as he is undoubtedly one of the best card-holders known to man. We are taking full advantage of a plethora of high cards when I pick up a hand as South which, in my case, is certainly not a welcome stranger:

Dealer West.   ♠ 8 7 6 5 4
Both Vul.   ♡ 8 5
                ◊ 10 4
                ♣ K 8 6 2

When West opens 1♣, my partner overcalls 1◊ and East bids 1♡. West jumps to 3♡ and East advances to game, leaving us with this brief collection of bids:

West	North	East	South
1♣	1◊	1♡	pass
3♡	pass	4♡	all pass

I dutifully lead the ◊10 and dummy is revealed:

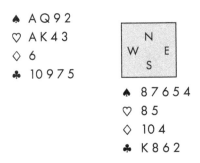

♠ A Q 9 2
♡ A K 4 3
◊ 6
♣ 10 9 7 5

♠ 8 7 6 5 4
♡ 8 5
◊ 10 4
♣ K 8 6 2

My partner wins with the ◊A, cashes the ♣A and continues with the ♣Q as I follow with the ♣8 and ♣2. At Trick 4 my partner plays the ◊2, but declarer plays the king, draws trumps and claims.

This was the layout:

```
                    ♠ 10 3
                    ♡ J 10
                    ◇ A Q 8 7 5 3 2
                    ♣ A Q
  ♠ A Q 9 2                              ♠ K J
  ♡ A K 4 3          N                   ♡ Q 9 7 6 2
  ◇ 6             W     E                ◇ K J 9
  ♣ 10 9 7 5         S                   ♣ J 4 3
                    ♠ 8 7 6 5 4
                    ♡ 8 5
                    ◇ 10 4
                    ♣ K 8 6 2
```

POST-MORTEM

I trust, having got this far in the book, that the reader realized that the winning play is for South to overtake the ♣Q with the king and play a third club for partner to ruff.

During the qualifying rounds of a pairs championship I find myself looking at this average collection as South:

Dealer East.
Both Vul.

♠ 8 5 2
♡ Q J 10 6
◇ A Q J
♣ 9 7 3

When East passes, I have nothing to say and West opens 1♠. East responds 1NT and then bids 2♠ over West's 2♣ rebid, which is enough to
see West jump to 4♠, giving us this auction:

West	North	East	South
		pass	pass
1♠	pass	1NT	pass
2♣	pass	2♠	pass
4♠	all pass		

My partner leads the ◇10:

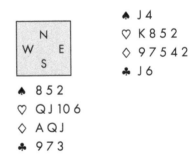

♠ J 4
♡ K 8 5 2
◇ 9 7 5 4 2
♣ J 6

♠ 8 5 2
♡ Q J 10 6
◇ A Q J
♣ 9 7 3

Having responded with a modest hand, a once frowned-upon strategy
that has now become de rigueur, East was obliged to give preference to
spades.

Dummy does not appear to be too threatening. Wanting to make
sure declarer cannot ruff clubs in dummy, I win with the ◇A and switch
to the ♠2. Partner wins with the ace and returns the ♠3, but declar-

er overtakes dummy's jack with the queen and plays a third round of trumps, partner following with the nine. When declarer plays the ♡3, partner goes up with the ace and plays a diamond, but declarer claims the rest, the ♡K taking care of a losing diamond when the ♣J proves to be an entry to dummy.

This was the layout:

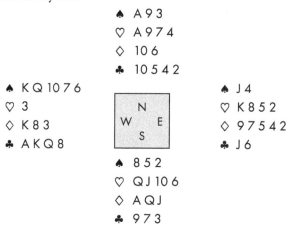

```
                    ♠ A 9 3
                    ♡ A 9 7 4
                    ◇ 10 6
                    ♣ 10 5 4 2
  ♠ K Q 10 7 6            N           ♠ J 4
  ♡ 3                 W       E       ♡ K 8 5 2
  ◇ K 8 3                 S           ◇ 9 7 5 4 2
  ♣ A K Q 8                           ♣ J 6
                    ♠ 8 5 2
                    ♡ Q J 10 6
                    ◇ A Q J
                    ♣ 9 7 3
```

POST-MORTEM

The lead of the ◇10 was likely to be from a doubleton, making declarer's probable distribution 5=1=3=4. If South calmly plays the ◇J at Trick 1, the defenders should not find it too difficult to take their top tricks, as long as North goes up with the ♡A and plays a second diamond.

Only a small number of pairs bid game with the East-West cards and the majority of those who did were unsuccessful.

When you know the opponents are in a hopeless contract that you have doubled, it is easy to take your eye off the ball and drop one or more tricks. During the qualifying rounds of a major pairs event, I pick up this hand as South:

Dealer West.   ♠ A 10
N-S Vul.   ♡ A J 8 5 3
                 ♢ 7 3 2
                 ♣ A 5 2

West has nothing to say, but when my partner opens 1♣ I alert and explain that it promises 16 or more points in the Precision style. That does not deter East, who enters the fray with a weak jump to 3♠. When I double (for takeout, showing 8+), West raises to 4♠ and that comes back to me. I am awkwardly placed, which is quite often the case when the bidding escalates quickly. I could bid 5♡, but that strikes me as speculative. I consider bidding 4NT, which might be fine if partner interprets it as natural, but he is all too likely to treat it as offering two places to play. I fall back on a double, knowing that partner will not play me for a massive holding in trumps. That ends proceedings:

West	North	East	South
pass	1♣*	3♠*	dbl*
4♠	pass	pass	dbl
all pass			

When you know your side holds the majority of the high cards, it can be a good idea to lead a trump, but it's possible that the ♠10 will be valuable and I don't want to waste it. I could lead one of my other aces to take a look at dummy, but eventually I settle for leading the ◇3. As I anticipated, there is not much in dummy:

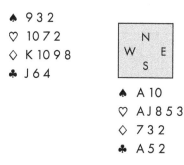

♠ 9 3 2
♡ 10 7 2
◇ K 10 9 8
♣ J 6 4

♠ A 10
♡ A J 8 5 3
◇ 7 3 2
♣ A 5 2

Partner plays the jack on dummy's eight; declarer wins with the queen and promptly plays the ◇5 to dummy's king. Partner wins with the ace and plays the ♡K, declarer following with the six as I give count with the ♡3. When partner continues with the ♡4, declarer ruffs, plays a diamond to dummy's ten and continues with the ◇9. When my partner ruffs that with the ♠J, declarer discards the ♣7 and I throw the ♣2. Partner continues with the ♣K followed by the ♣3 — I win that and exit with a heart. Declarer ruffs and plays the ♠K, claiming the rest when I win with the ace. That adds up to three down, -500.

This was the distribution:

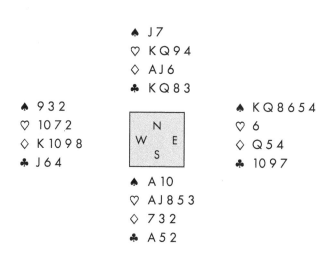

♠ J 7
♡ K Q 9 4
◇ A J 6
♣ K Q 8 3

♠ 9 3 2
♡ 10 7 2
◇ K 10 9 8
♣ J 6 4

♠ K Q 8 6 5 4
♡ 6
◇ Q 5 4
♣ 10 9 7

♠ A 10
♡ A J 8 5 3
◇ 7 3 2
♣ A 5 2

My diamond lead was unlucky, but should not have affected the outcome. I should have overtaken the ♣K and returned the five. Partner then plays a third round of the suit, which will ensure I score two trump tricks — if declarer ruffs with an honor, I simply discard a heart.

More significant was declarer's decision to ruff the second heart. If he discards a club, a loser-on-loser, he removes the possibility of the defenders obtaining a trump promotion.

Having scored a heart trick, my partner should have turned his attention to clubs — playing four rounds of the suit will again deliver the promotion.

Despite the fact that our opponents scored well, it strikes me that their bidding was risky — East ought to have a seventh spade, and West's raise with a flat hand was hardly gilt-edged. However, it reflects the way the game is played in the 21st century.

With our side cold for eleven tricks in notrump, hearts or even clubs, +500 was a dreadful result. But I was right about the ♠10.

It is easy enough to imagine that the defense starts with the opening lead, but the reality is somewhat different. It is often possible to obtain a significant clue from the bids that were — or were not — made. Playing in an important team championship, I pick up these cards as South:

Dealer West. ♠ 7
Neither Vul. ♡ K 10 6 3
♢ A Q 4
♣ K 9 7 6 2

After two passes, the player on my right opens 1♠ and I double. West now bids 2♡, which is explained as showing a good raise to 2♠. When my partner doubles, East jumps to 4♠. I have nothing to contribute but my partner now bids 5♢ and that prompts East to keep going with 5♠, which brings this competitive auction to a close.

West	North	East	South
pass	pass	1♠	dbl
2♡*	dbl	4♠	pass
pass	5♢	5♠	all pass

Placing partner with a good suit I lead the ♢A:

♠ K 10 5
♡ J 9 5
♢ 8 7 6
♣ A 10 8 3

♠ 7
♡ K 10 6 3
♢ A Q 4
♣ K 9 7 6 2

Partner encourages with the ♢10 and I continue with the ♢Q. However, declarer ruffs that, cashes the ♠AQ on which I pitch the ♡6, and then advances the ♣J. I don't fall into the trap of covering, and partner wins with the queen and switches to the ♡2. Declarer wins with the ace and plays a club to dummy's eight. When partner discards a diamond, he ruffs a diamond and plays a club to the ten, the ♣A taking care of the losing heart.

This was the layout:

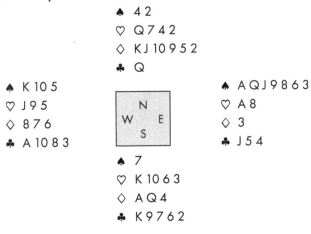

```
                    ♠ 4 2
                    ♡ Q 7 4 2
                    ◇ K J 10 9 5 2
                    ♣ Q
    ♠ K 10 5                        ♠ A Q J 9 8 6 3
    ♡ J 9 5            N            ♡ A 8
    ◇ 8 7 6       W       E         ◇ 3
    ♣ A 10 8 3        S            ♣ J 5 4
                    ♠ 7
                    ♡ K 10 6 3
                    ◇ A Q 4
                    ♣ K 9 7 6 2
```

POST-MORTEM

In order to be sure of defeating the contract, South must switch to a heart at Trick 2. It was clear that partner's double of 2♡ showed length in that suit. When he subsequently jumped to 5◇, South should have realized that bid was based on a six-card suit. With, say, four hearts and only five diamonds partner could have bid 4NT over 4♠, suggesting two places to play, and plannng to retreat to 5◇ if I bid 5♣. It was, as Sherlock Holmes might have said, 'a case of the dog that didn't bark in the night'.

Declarer's play in the club suit was immaculate, offering a 26.58% chance of three tricks. In the other room, North opened with a weak 2◇ and, although South raised to 4◇, East was allowed to play in 4♠.

POINTLESS EXERCISE

52

Little has been written about the best seating strategy when playing long knockout matches. Suppose you start strongly and have the chance to play against the same opponents in the next set? My advice would be to forgo the opportunity. If the match becomes close, it may be to your advantage to have played against at least one of the opponent's other pairs. After making significant gains in the first set of a match, my partner has insisted we continue against the same opponents when I pick up this poor selection as South:

Dealer West.
Both Vul.

♠ Q J 9 8 3
♡ 5 4
◇ J 6 4 3
♣ 4 3

When West opens 1◇, my partner overcalls 1NT. However, East waves the Stop card before bidding 4♡, leaving us with this one-round sequence:

West	North	East	South
1◇	1NT	4♡	all pass

With little to go on, I reluctantly opt for the ♠Q. That is usually a precursor for dummy holding something like ♠K105 and declarer ♠A6, but this time it is not quite so bad:

♠ K 5 2
♡ A
◇ A Q 10 8 2
♣ Q J 10 8

```
      N
  W       E
      S
```

♠ Q J 9 8 3
♡ 5 4
◇ J 6 4 3
♣ 4 3

Declarer plays low from dummy, partner following with the four and de-clarer the seven. When I continue with the jack of spades, declarer plays dummy's king; partner wins with the ace and returns the ♠10. Declarer ruffs and plays a club to the queen and ace. My partner immediately re-turns the ♣5, but declarer matches him for speed by discarding the ◇5, soon claiming the remaining tricks.

This was the layout:

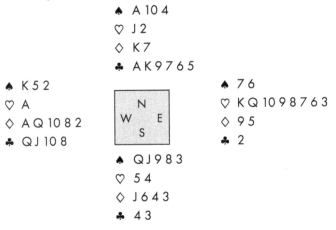

```
              ♠ A 10 4
              ♡ J 2
              ◇ K 7
              ♣ A K 9 7 6 5
♠ K 5 2                          ♠ 7 6
♡ A              N               ♡ K Q 10 9 8 7 6 3
◇ A Q 10 8 2  W     E            ◇ 9 5
♣ Q J 10 8       S               ♣ 2
              ♠ Q J 9 8 3
              ♡ 5 4
              ◇ J 6 4 3
              ♣ 4 3
```

POST-MORTEM

Suppose North exits with a heart at Trick 3. Declarer wins in dummy, ruffs a spade and runs all her trumps to reach a three-card ending. If North comes down to a singleton club honor, she will be thrown in with it and if she blanks the ◇K, declarer will be able to drop it.

To be sure of defeating 4♡, South must switch to a diamond at Trick 2. Assuming the defense are going to score two spade tricks, the other two must come from the remaining suits. On lead for the last time, the combination of North's overcall and East's jump to game make me think this should not have been beyond me.

In the other room North overcalled 2♣ rather than 1NT, and South led the ♣4 against 4♡. North won with the ace and returned a heart. Having taken dummy's ace, declarer played the ♣J, covered and ruffed, drew trumps and played a diamond to the queen and king. North could take the ♠A but declarer had the rest, +420 and no swing.

WAKE-UP CALL

53

During an invitational pairs event where my role is supposed to be that of VuGraph commentator, I am temporarily called into action when one of the players feels unwell. With no time for any significant discussion other than that we will play Precision, I pick up this hand as South:

Dealer North.	♠ Q J 7 5 4
Neither Vul.	♡ 7
	◇ Q 3
	♣ K J 5 4 3

When my partner opens 1♡, East doubles and when I bid 1♠, West is there with 2◇. My partner's pass sees East continue with 2♡ and, when West rebids 3◇, she tries 3NT. West considers for a moment and then jumps to 5◇, giving us this auction:

West	North	East	South
	1♡	dbl	1♠
2◇	pass	2♡	pass
3◇	pass	3NT	pass
5◇	all pass		

My partner leads the ♡K:

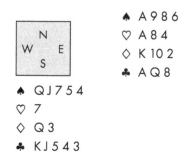

♠ A 9 8 6
♡ A 8 4
◇ K 10 2
♣ A Q 8

♠ Q J 7 5 4
♡ 7
◇ Q 3
♣ K J 5 4 3

I am great believer that with a balanced hand you bid notrump, so I would overcall 1NT rather than double with the East cards, secure in the knowledge that partner will have a fair idea of what I have.

Declarer wins with dummy's ♡A, plays a spade to the king and then advances the ◊5, which partner wins with the ace. After cashing the ♡K and ♡Q, on which I discard my black fives, partner switches to the ♣10 and declarer takes dummy's ace, cashes the ◊K and claims the rest for one down.

The layout:

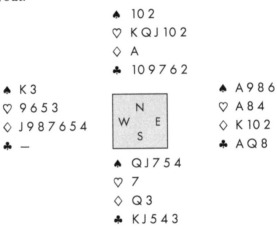

```
              ♠ 10 2
              ♡ K Q J 10 2
              ◊ A
              ♣ 10 9 7 6 2
♠ K 3                          ♠ A 9 8 6
♡ 9 6 5 3         N            ♡ A 8 4
◊ J 9 8 7 6 5 4  W   E         ◊ K 10 2
♣ —               S            ♣ A Q 8
              ♠ Q J 7 5 4
              ♡ 7
              ◊ Q 3
              ♣ K J 5 4 3
```

POST-MORTEM

We scored only 40% on this deal. If partner had played a fourth round of hearts, my ◊Q would have been promoted. Had I been awake, I would have discarded the ♣K on one of the hearts to alert partner to the possibility.

If West had bid only 4◊ it would have been essential to find the trump promotion, as -130 would have been an absolute zero.

BALANCING ACT

54

Playing bridge affords one the opportunity of traveling the world — early in the year one can compete in major events in Japan and Australia. Having made the long trip from the UK, we have reached the final stages of one of the team events when I pick up these cards as South:

Dealer South.	♠ K J 9 8 5
Neither Vul.	♡ 9 7 6 3
	◊ 7 2
	♣ A 3

Under certain circumstances I might consider opening my hand, but none of them exist here. After I pass, West opens 1♡, promising four or more hearts. When East raises to 2♡ I can place partner with a shortage in the suit, and I now venture 2♠. When this gets back to East he doubles, and I have an anxious moment before West bids 2NT, which ends the auction:

West	North	East	South
			pass
1♡	pass	2♡	2♠
pass	pass	dbl	pass
2NT	all pass		

My partner leads the ♠6 and dummy is about what I expected:

	♠ A 10
	♡ A 8 2
N	◊ 9 8 5 4 3
W E	♣ Q 7 5
S	
♠ K J 9 8 5	
♡ 9 7 6 3	
◊ 7 2	
♣ A 3	

When declarer plays dummy's ten, I consider putting in the ♠J, which would be a possibility if I thought partner had only two spades. However, holding four spades to the queen, West might have converted his partner's double, making it likely that partner has three cards in the suit. I win with the king and return the ♠5. Declarer, who has followed with the ♠2 and ♠3, wins with dummy's ace as partner plays the ♠7, and then plays a diamond to the king. When that holds, he continues with the queen; partner wins and plays the ♠4. Declarer wins with the queen, cashes the ◇J, crosses to the ♡A and takes the two established diamonds. I discard a heart on the third round of diamonds followed by a club and second heart. Declarer now plays a heart and, having observed partner's ♡10 on the first round of the suit, now plays the king, which gives him four heart tricks and ten in total.

This was the unfortunate layout:

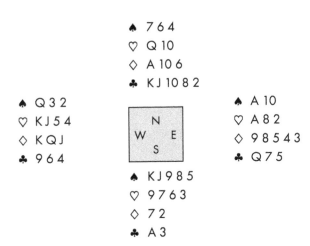

```
                    ♠ 7 6 4
                    ♡ Q 10
                    ◇ A 10 6
                    ♣ K J 10 8 2
      ♠ Q 3 2                        ♠ A 10
      ♡ K J 5 4          N           ♡ A 8 2
      ◇ K Q J       W        E       ◇ 9 8 5 4 3
      ♣ 9 6 4           S           ♣ Q 7 5
                    ♠ K J 9 8 5
                    ♡ 9 7 6 3
                    ◇ 7 2
                    ♣ A 3
```

The winning defense was not difficult to find. Having won the first spade, all South had to do was to play two rounds of clubs. That only requires partner to have five clubs headed by the king and an outside entry.

You have doubtless realized that declarer missed an opportunity — if he goes up with dummy's ♠A at Trick 1 and plays on diamonds, he cannot be defeated.

In the other room South was able to open 2♡ to show a weak hand with both majors (a method explained in The Mysterious Multi), and North played in 2♠, which made on the nose.

Playing in one of the many invitational events that are scattered across the bridge calendar, my partner is first-class, as are the opponents. In the middle of a match in the round-robin, I pick up this hand as South:

Dealer East.	♠ J 10 6 2
Neither Vul.	♡ —
	♦ A J 9 3 2
	♣ J 10 9 6

When East passes, I have nothing to say and West opens 2♣, promising a strong hand. East responds with a 'waiting' 2♦ and I take the opportunity to insert a double. When West rebids 2♡, my partner gets into the auction with 3♦. East doubles that for penalties, but West is not interested and jumps to 4♡. That does not end proceedings as East now bids 4♠, which is clearly a cuebid in support of hearts. When West continues with 5♣ my partner doubles, and when East passes, West redoubles to indicate he has first-round control in clubs. East bids 5♡, but West is not finished and advances to 6♡, leaving us with this lengthy auction:

West	North	East	South
		pass	pass
2♣*	pass	2♦*	dbl
2♡	3♦	dbl	pass
4♡	pass	4♠*	pass
5♣*	dbl	pass	pass
redbl*	pass	5♡	pass
6♡	all pass		

My partner leads the ◊6 and dummy is revealed:

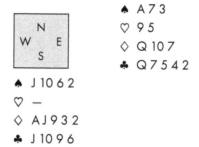

	♠ A 7 3
	♡ 9 5
	◊ Q 10 7
	♣ Q 7 5 4 2

♠ J 10 6 2
♡ —
◊ A J 9 3 2
♣ J 10 9 6

I put up the ace and declarer follows with the king. Recalling partner's double, I switch to the ♣J. Declarer wins with the ace, crosses to dummy with the ♡9 and discards the ♣8 on the ◊Q. That is followed by another seven hearts, partner following to the first three. As the last one settles on the table, this is the situation:

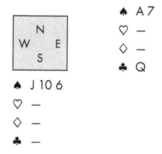

	♠ A 7
	♡ —
	◊ —
	♣ Q

♠ J 10 6
♡ —
◊ —
♣ —

When my partner discards the ♠9, declarer throws dummy's ♣Q and then plays the ♠8 from his hand. When partner's king appears, the last trick goes to declarer's ♠Q.

The full deal:

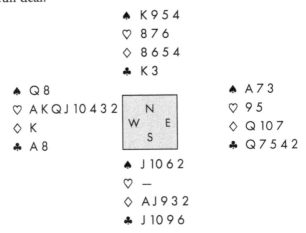

                ♠ K 9 5 4
                ♡ 8 7 6
                ◇ 8 6 5 4
                ♣ K 3

♠ Q 8   ♠ A 7 3
♡ A K Q J 10 4 3 2   ♡ 9 5
◇ K   ◇ Q 10 7
♣ A 8   ♣ Q 7 5 4 2

                ♠ J 10 6 2
                ♡ —
                ◇ A J 9 3 2
                ♣ J 10 9 6

POST-MORTEM

This was the situation as declarer cashed the last heart:

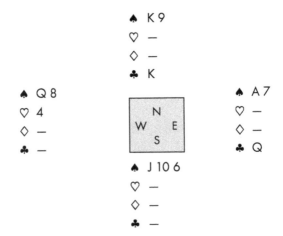

                ♠ K 9
                ♡ —
                ◇ —
                ♣ K

♠ Q 8   ♠ A 7
♡ 4   ♡ —
◇ —   ◇ —
♣ —   ♣ Q

                ♠ J 10 6
                ♡ —
                ◇ —
                ♣ —

Having taken a trick with the ◇A, it was pointless to switch to a club. The standard defense in this type of situation is to attack the potential entry to dummy. If South switches to a spade at Trick 2, declarer must go down.

At the other table, the contract was 4♡. When North led the ♠5, declarer went up with dummy's ace and played a diamond. South pounced on that with the ace and returned the ♠J to North's king, but that was the last trick for the defense, +450.

Over a period of time one may discover that one has proffered conflicting advice pertaining to certain areas of the game. One such area surrounds the question of entering the auction in a pairs game. The idea that one must try to bid whenever possible conflicts with the fact that when you know you are outgunned it may merely serve to aid declarer during the play. The quandary came to mind on this deal from a club duplicate where my partner's major contribution so far is that he knows where the bar is located. I am South, and pick up this hand

Dealer West.   ♠ J 6
Both Vul.   ♡ J 8
             ◇ A K J 7 5
             ♣ Q 9 7 6

West opens 1♠ and East responds 2♡. It would not be ridiculous to double now, but at this vulnerability a profitable sacrifice is unlikely. Overcalling 3◇ might help partner if he is on lead, but it is not without risk and, as it is clear that the opponents hold the balance of power, I go quietly and pass. When West rebids 2♠, East continues with 3♣ and West bids 3♡. After a brief pause for thought East bids 4◇, which is clearly a cuebid based on a shortage. I could double that, but if the bid is based on a void, East will be able to show a first-round control by redoubling; in any event I will be on lead against a likely heart contract. When I pass, West bids 5♣ and that is enough for East to jump to 6♡. This was the sequence:

West	North	East	South
1♠	pass	2♡	pass
2♠	pass	3♣	pass
3♡	pass	4◇*	pass
5♣	pass	6♡	all pass

I lead the ◇K, which in our methods asks partner to give count.

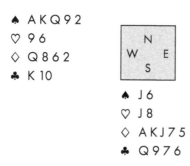

♠ AKQ92
♡ 96
◇ Q862
♣ K 10

♠ J 6
♡ J 8
◇ A K J 7 5
♣ Q 9 7 6

Partner follows with the ◇3 and declarer the ◇4. Clearly, declarer has a singleton diamond, but I can't be totally sure about his distribution aside from the fact that he must have at least five hearts and four clubs. Given that declarer did not ask for keycards, I don't think he has any worries about the trump suit, so with the idea of cutting down possible club ruffs in dummy I exit with the ♡J. Declarer wins with the ace, and after some thought plays three more rounds of hearts, partner following with the ♡2, ♡4, ♡5 and ♡7. Declarer now plays three rounds of spades, discarding a club on the third round, ruffs a spade and cashes his remaining trump to reach this position:

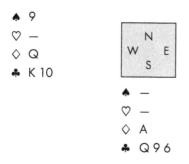

♠ 9
♡ —
◇ Q
♣ K 10

♠ —
♡ —
◇ A
♣ Q 9 6

Declarer now crosses to dummy with the ♣K and cashes the ♠9, which squeezes me in the minors.

This was the full deal:

```
                    ♠ 10 8 4 3
                    ♡ 7 5 4 2
                    ◇ 10 9 3
                    ♣ J 4
    ♠ A K Q 9 2                        ♠ 7 5
    ♡ 9 6              N                ♡ A K Q 10 3
    ◇ Q 8 6 2       W     E            ◇ 4
    ♣ K 10             S                ♣ A 8 5 3 2
                    ♠ J 6
                    ♡ J 8
                    ◇ A K J 7 5
                    ♣ Q 9 7 6
```

POST-MORTEM

My analysis was sound — as far as it went. If declarer is credited with five trump tricks, three top spades and two clubs, it is clear that an extra trick can be established by ruffing a spade. (North might have five spades, but that will inevitably mean declarer has six hearts.) Once you reach that conclusion it should not be impossible to find a club switch at Trick 2, which destroys declarer's communications. Amusingly, you can lead any of your four clubs!

It was only towards the end of the 1980s that the Defense of the Realm Act in the United Kingdom was modified to allow public houses to remain open after 10.30 at night. In our unlicensed club, that meant that on occasion dummy had to sprint to the hostelry around the corner to get the drinks in before the traditional call of 'Time, gentlemen please!'. With the clock showing 10.20, I pick up this modest collection as South:

Dealer South.	♠ Q J 9
Both Vul.	♡ 4
	◇ J 10 9 8 4
	♣ K Q 8 2

I briefly consider starting with a weak 2◇, but the vulnerability argues against it, as does the fact that we are playing Multi. When I pass, West opens 1♣ and when his partner responds 1◇, promising a heart suit, he rebids 1♠. That sees East jump to 3NT, leaving this auction:

West	North	East	South
			pass
1♣	pass	1◇*	pass
1♠	pass	3NT	all pass

I look no further than the ◊J and I see that I have hit dummy's weakness:

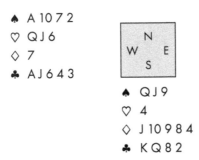

♠ A 10 7 2
♡ Q J 6
◊ 7
♣ A J 6 4 3

♠ Q J 9
♡ 4
◊ J 10 9 8 4
♣ K Q 8 2

My partner wins with the ◊A and returns the ◊2. Declarer, after following with the ◊6, wins Trick 2 with the king and plays the ♡8 to the four, queen and ace. Partner continues with the ◊3 and declarer wins with the queen, plays a heart to dummy's jack and a heart back to the king to leave these cards:

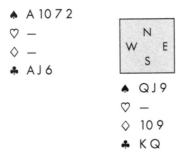

♠ A 10 7 2
♡ —
◊ —
♣ A J 6

♠ Q J 9
♡ —
◊ 10 9
♣ K Q

When declarer plays the ♡10, I realize I am in trouble, as declarer must have the ♠K. I try discarding a diamond, but declarer plays a club to the queen and ace and returns the ♣J. I can win and cash a diamond, but declarer claims the rest.

This was the layout:

```
              ♠ 8 5 4 3
              ♡ A 7 5 3 2
              ◇ A 5 3 2
              ♣ —
♠ A 10 7 2                      ♠ K 6
♡ Q J 6         ┌─────────┐     ♡ K 10 9 8
◇ 7            │    N    │     ◇ K Q 6
♣ A J 6 4 3    │ W     E │     ♣ 10 9 7 5
               │    S    │
               └─────────┘
              ♠ Q J 9
              ♡ 4
              ◇ J 10 9 8 4
              ♣ K Q 8 2
```

POST-MORTEM

My mistake was a common one. I must keep the ◇4, maintaining a line of communication to North's hand. Now after I win a trick with the ♣K, a diamond switch allows North to win and cash the last heart.

Elimination play is one of the strongest weapons in declarer's armory. From a defender's point of view communications can be all-important, whether it be with regard to maintaining a link with partner, or severing a connection between declarer and dummy. During a regular duplicate at the club I pick up this hand as South:

Dealer North.　　　♠ J 9 2
N-S Vul.　　　　　♡ K Q 10 7 3
　　　　　　　　　◊ 6
　　　　　　　　　♣ 10 9 5 3

When my partner passes, East opens 1◊. Following my own philosophy that playing pairs one must try to bid if at all possible, I overcall 1♡ — and then remember that the scoring in this event is IMPs. West bids 2♡, which could be based on various hands, and my partner's pass indicates that he does not have a high heart honor. East jumps to 3NT and West now bids 4◊, which turns out be asking for keycards. East's reply of 5♣ shows 2 keycards and the ◊Q, and that is enough for West to jump to 6◊. This is the auction:

West	North	East	South
	pass	1◊	1♡
2♡*	pass*	3NT	pass
4◊*	pass	5♣*	pass
6◊	all pass		

I lead the ♡K and dummy is not short of controls:

♠ A K 7
♡ A 5 2
◊ J 10 7 3
♣ A 6 4

　　　　　　　♠ J 9 2
　　　　　　　♡ K Q 10 7 3
　　　　　　　◊ 6
　　　　　　　♣ 10 9 5 3

Dummy's ace takes the trick, partner following with the six and declarer the eight. Declarer plays dummy's ◇J and that holds the trick as my partner follows with the ◇4. A diamond to the queen sees partner play the two while I discard the ♡3. When declarer continues with the diamond ace, I discard the ♠2 and partner follows with the ◇9. Declarer cashes the ♣KQ, crosses to dummy with a spade, throws a heart on the ♣A and plays the ♠K, followed by the seven. When partner plays the ♠Q, declarer discards the ♡9 and partner, left with the ♠106 and the ♣J, has to offer up a ruff and discard, allowing declarer to dispose of a losing heart.

This was the full deal:

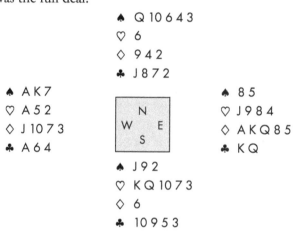

```
                    ♠  Q 10 6 4 3
                    ♡  6
                    ◇  9 4 2
                    ♣  J 8 7 2
    ♠  A K 7                            ♠  8 5
    ♡  A 5 2          N                 ♡  J 9 8 4
    ◇  J 10 7 3   W       E             ◇  A K Q 8 5
    ♣  A 6 4          S                 ♣  K Q
                    ♠  J 9 2
                    ♡  K Q 10 7 3
                    ◇  6
                    ♣  10 9 5 3
```

POST-MORTEM

My mistake was to discard a spade, exposing North to a loser-on-loser play.

They reached 6◇ in the other room, but South made no mistake.

When the long-defunct European Bridge magazine asked a group of experts how the average player might hope to improve, they were virtually unanimous that a combination of reading and playing against strong opponents was essential. It is tempting to think that there can be nothing new to write about the game, but every few years a modern classic appears. Studying such works can seriously improve your game. In a major championship I hold the following:

> Dealer West. ♠ A 10 7 2
> N-S Vul.   ♡ 4
>   ♢ 7 6 2
>   ♣ Q 10 6 5 3

After a couple of passes, East opens 2NT and West bids 3♣, hoping to find a major-suit fit. When East responds 3♢ he denies a five-card major; that is enough to see West bring the sequence to a close with 3NT.

West	North	East	South
pass	pass	2NT	pass
3♣*	pass	3♢*	pass
3NT	all pass		

I look no further than my longest suit and lead the ♣5 to reveal this dummy:

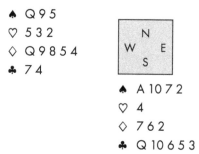

```
            ♠ Q 9 5
            ♡ 5 3 2          N
            ◇ Q 9 8 5 4   W     E
            ♣ 7 4            S
                          ♠ A 10 7 2
                          ♡ 4
                          ◇ 7 6 2
                          ♣ Q 10 6 5 3
```

Declarer calls for dummy's four and the best partner can do is the eight, which loses to the ♣9. Declarer continues with the ◇K, which holds the trick as I follow with the two and partner the three. The next card is the ◇J and partner wins with the ace and returns the ♣2. Declarer plays the ♣A and follows it with the ♠3. When I follow with the ♠7, declarer puts in dummy's nine; partner wins with the king and switches to the ♡10. Declarer plays the jack and when that holds he plays a spade. There is no way to prevent declarer reaching dummy's diamonds and he is soon claiming ten tricks.

This was the full deal:

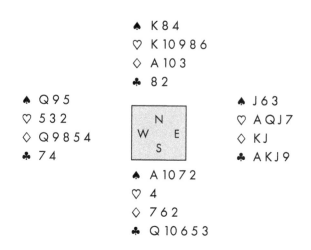

```
                  ♠ K 8 4
                  ♡ K 10 9 8 6
                  ◇ A 10 3
                  ♣ 8 2
  ♠ Q 9 5                          ♠ J 6 3
  ♡ 5 3 2            N             ♡ A Q J 7
  ◇ Q 9 8 5 4    W     E          ◇ K J
  ♣ 7 4              S             ♣ A K J 9
                  ♠ A 10 7 2
                  ♡ 4
                  ◇ 7 6 2
                  ♣ Q 10 6 5 3
```

South should realize that North must have the ♠K to have won the second diamond. If East leads a low spade, South must insert the ten! (It is also possible to fly up with the ace the first time provided you intend to play the ten when declarer plays another low spade.) North-South are then in a position to deny declarer an entry to dummy. If East starts with the ♠J, both defenders duck. Finally, if declarer leads a low spade and South has an honor without the ten, he must fly up with the honor in case declarer has ♠J10x.

All of which goes to prove that there are more things than are contemplated in — at least — my philosophy.

In the other room, they also reached 3NT and the early play was identical. When North ducked the second round of diamonds, declarer played a spade and once again South failed to put in the ten. North took the nine with the king and returned a club, but declarer won and played a second spade, South winning and exiting with a spade. Declarer won in dummy, played a heart to the jack and exited with the ♡7. North could win and cash the ◇A, but then had to lead into the ♡AQ.

Anyone who has read *The Rodwell Files* should have a much better chance of finding the winning play(s).

Even very strong opponents are capable of making mistakes. The difficulty lies in spotting the opportunities that arise. Playing in a knockout event with a sponsor against a pair of world champions, I pick up as South:

Dealer East.	♠ K 9 8
E-W Vul.	♡ 9 3 2
	◇ K
	♣ J 10 6 5 4 2

When East opens 1♠, I flirt with the idea of overcalling 3♣ before sanity prevails, and West responds with a game-forcing 2♡. East raises to 3♡ and West cuebids 4♣. When East replies with a cuebid of 4◇, West bids 4♡, but East continues with 4♠, which sees West bid 5♣ before going on to 6♡ over East's 5♡. This has been the auction:

West	North	East	South
		1♠	pass
2♡*	pass	3♡	pass
4♣*	pass	4◇*	pass
4♡	pass	4♠*	pass
5♣*	pass	5♡	pass
6♡	all pass		

My partner leads the ♡4 and dummy proves to have a shapely minimum:

♠ A J 7 3 2
♡ Q 8 6
◇ A 7 5 4 2
♣ —

```
              ♠ A J 7 3 2
        N     ♡ Q 8 6
      W   E   ◇ A 7 5 4 2
        S     ♣ —

♠ K 9 8
♡ 9 3 2
◇ K
♣ J 10 6 5 4 2
```

When I follow with the two, declarer wins with the seven, ruffs a club, overtakes the ♡Q and plays another top heart. Partner, having followed to the club with the seven, now discards the ♣9. Declarer runs the ◊Q to my king and I exit with the ♣J. Saving time, declarer shows his hand and claims. This was the distribution:

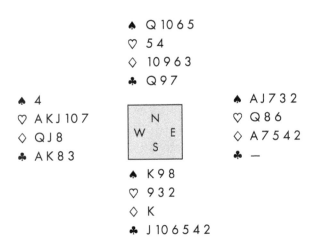

```
                     ♠ Q 10 6 5
                     ♡ 5 4
                     ◊ 10 9 6 3
                     ♣ Q 9 7
      ♠ 4                              ♠ A J 7 3 2
      ♡ A K J 10 7      N              ♡ Q 8 6
      ◊ Q J 8       W       E          ◊ A 7 5 4 2
      ♣ A K 8 3         S              ♣ —
                     ♠ K 9 8
                     ♡ 9 3 2
                     ◊ K
                     ♣ J 10 6 5 4 2
```

POST-MORTEM

Declarer explains he can win the club, test the diamonds, ruff the fourth round and then return to dummy with the ♠A, the long diamond taking care of his losing club (what's more he can score the last trick with the ◊7!). It dawns on me that I could have upset the applecart by returning a low spade, removing a vital entry to dummy.

In the other room they reached the same contract and the play was identical. However, when he gained the lead with the ◊K my counterpart switched to the ♠8 to win 17 IMPs.

Suppose declarer runs the ◊Q at Trick 2 and South wins and returns a heart? Declarer wins, crosses to the ♠A, ruffs a spade, ruffs a club, ruffs a spade, draws the outstanding trump, and cashes the ◊J. When South discards, declarer cashes the top clubs, and North, down to ♠Q ◊10 9, is squeezed.

The legendary Italian champion, Giorgio Belladonna, maintained that one could become a good player without any real knowledge of squeeze play. That is perhaps possible, but a defender must stay alive to the possibility that they or partner might come under pressure as the hand unfolds. In the last round of a one-day event, our team is already assured of victory when I pick up this hand as South:

Dealer East.	♠ Q 6
Neither Vul.	♡ J 9 3
	◇ K 10 8
	♣ Q 8 6 5 2

East opens 1◇, promising a five-card suit or a 4=4=4=1 hand. When West responds 1♠, East jumps to 4♣, showing a singleton or void in a hand worth 16-17 points in support of spades. That is enough for West to ask for keycards, East showing 0 or 3 with 5◇. When West enquires about the ♠Q with 5♡, East denies it and West now bids 6◇, offering East a choice of slams. After brief consideration, East passes, giving us this sequence:

West	North	East	South
		1◇*	pass
1♠	pass	4♣*	pass
4NT*	pass	5◇*	pass
5♡*	pass	5♠*	pass
6◇	all pass		

My diamonds appear to be well-placed and it will be a big surprise if I don't have at least one trump trick. A spade lead is out of the question, so my choice is between hearts and clubs. It seems to me that a club must be the safest option and I start with the ♣5:

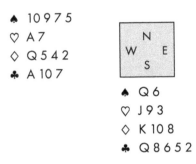

♠ 10 9 7 5
♡ A 7
◇ Q 5 4 2
♣ A 10 7

♠ Q 6
♡ J 9 3
◇ K 10 8
♣ Q 8 6 5 2

The bidding marks declarer with the ♠AK and the ◇A and he must have the ♡K along with some additional high cards.

Declarer wins with dummy's ace, ruffs a club with the ◇7 and continues with the ◇9. I don't see any advantage in taking this, so I follow with the eight. After winning with dummy's queen, declarer ruffs a club with the ◇J, cashes the ◇A, crosses to dummy with a heart and exits with a diamond, discarding the ♠2 as partner throws the ♣K to match my ◇K. Declarer is out of trumps, so it must be safe to exit with a club, removing dummy's last trump. These cards remain:

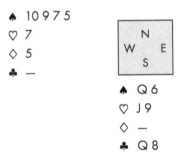

♠ 10 9 7 5
♡ 7
◇ 5
♣ —

♠ Q 6
♡ J 9
◇ —
♣ Q 8

When I play the club, declarer ruffs in dummy and partner considers for a while before pitching the ♡5. Declarer throws the ♠4 and proceeds to cash the ♠AK followed by the ♡KQ, the last trick being taken by declarer's ♡8.

This was the full deal:

```
                      ♠ J 8 3
                      ♡ 10 6 5 4
                      ◇ 6 3
                      ♣ K J 4 3
  ♠ 10 9 7 5                           ♠ A K 4 2
  ♡ A 7              N                  ♡ K Q 8 2
  ◇ Q 5 4 2     W         E            ◇ A J 9 7
  ♣ A 10 7          S                  ♣ 9
                      ♠ Q 6
                      ♡ J 9 3
                      ◇ K 10 8
                      ♣ Q 8 6 5 2
```

POST-MORTEM

This was the fatal ending:

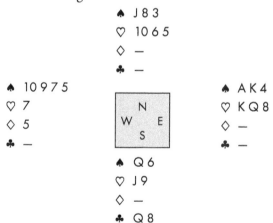

```
                      ♠ J 8 3
                      ♡ 10 6 5
                      ◇ —
                      ♣ —
  ♠ 10 9 7 5                           ♠ A K 4
  ♡ 7                N                  ♡ K Q 8
  ◇ 5           W         E            ◇ —
  ♣ —                S                  ♣ —
                      ♠ Q 6
                      ♡ J 9
                      ◇ —
                      ♣ Q 8
```

Playing a club inflicted a suicide squeeze on my partner. Exiting with a spade is no good, as declarer will be able to score three tricks in the suit, but exiting with a heart ensures one more trick for the defense. That should not have been difficult to see and neither should the play of winning with the ◇K when declarer played the ◇9. Then I can exit with a trump and declarer must lose another trick.

In the other room our teammates also reached 6◇ and a club was led. Declarer took the ace, ruffed a club, crossed to the ♡A, ruffed a club, cashed the ◇A and the ♡KQ and then played the ◇J. When my hand ducked, declarer found the essential play of overtaking the jack with dummy's queen and exiting with a diamond. Unable to touch spades, South played a club, but once again that squeezed North in the majors, so there was no swing.

Long Duel

Forcing the defenders to make several discards was a strategy favored by Maurice Harrison-Grey and also suggested as a Bols Bridge Tip by Patrick Jourdain. Even if the defenders discard correctly, they may not be out of the woods. On this deal from an early round of the Gold Cup, my team is well ahead when I pick up these cards as South:

Dealer South.	♠ K Q 8 7 3
N-S Vul.	♡ J
	♢ 8 6
	♣ Q 9 5 3 2

I consider opening 2♠, which in our methods would promise a weak hand with five spades, four or more cards in a minor and 5-10 points, and were the vulnerability reversed I would not hesitate to do so. West matches my pass, but my partner opens 3♡, which sees East bid 3NT, ending the auction:

West	North	East	South
			pass
pass	3♡	3NT	all pass

A third-hand preempt at this vulnerability could be quite strong, so I do not hesitate to lead partner's suit and put the ♡J on the table:

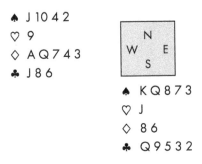

♠ J 10 4 2
♡ 9
◇ A Q 7 4 3
♣ J 8 6

♠ K Q 8 7 3
♡ J
◇ 8 6
♣ Q 9 5 3 2

Partner overtakes the jack with the queen and, when that holds, he continues with the ♡8, which declarer wins with the ace as I discard the ♣2 and dummy the ◇3. Declarer continues with a diamond to the queen, partner following with the nine, and cashes the ◇A, on which partner throws the ♡2. When declarer takes three more rounds of diamonds, partner discards the three and four of hearts and the ♠6. I am tempted to pitch two clubs and spade, but worried that declarer might have ♣AKx, I keep three cards in both spades and clubs to reach this position:

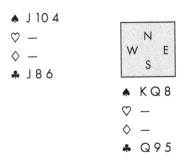

♠ J 10 4
♡ —
◇ —
♣ J 8 6

♠ K Q 8
♡ —
◇ —
♣ Q 9 5

Declarer cashes the ♠A and exits with a spade, partner discarding the ♡10. When I cash the ♠K, partner throws the ♣4 and declarer the ♡6. I exit with the ♣5 and when declarer plays dummy's six, partner produces the king. Declarer wins with the ace and returns the ♣10. I can take my queen, but have to surrender the game-going trick to dummy's ♣J.

The full deal:

```
                    ♠ 9 6
                    ♡ K Q 10 8 4 3 2
                    ◇ 9
                    ♣ K 7 4
♠ J 10 4 2                              ♠ A 5
♡ 9                    ┌─────────┐      ♡ A 7 6 5
◇ A Q 7 4 3           │    N    │      ◇ K J 10 5 2
♣ J 8 6               │ W     E │      ♣ A 10
                      │    S    │
                      └─────────┘
                    ♠ K Q 8 7 3
                    ♡ J
                    ◇ 8 6
                    ♣ Q 9 5 3 2
```

POST-MORTEM

The contract could have been defeated in several ways. If I infer from partner's play of the ♡8 followed by the order of the heart discards that he has the ♣K, I can safely come down to two clubs and four spades. And right at the end I missed another simple point — if I exit with the ♣Q rather than the ♣5 we must come to two more tricks, a play that was found in the other room.

Playing in a Swiss Teams event in Yorkshire with a famous married couple as teammates, I pick up these cards in the South seat:

Dealer South.   ♠ A K Q 9 6
N-S Vul.   ♡ K 3
                 ♢ J 8 3
                 ♣ 10 7 3

We are playing Precision, so my opening bid of 1♠ promises a maximum of 15 points. When West overcalls with a weak 3♢, my partner competes with 3♠. That is not enough to silence East and his 4♣ brings the auction to an end:

West	North	East	South
			1♠
3♢	3♠	4♣	all pass

We are experimenting with defensive methods that are popular with leading European experts, leading second and fourth (so low from a small doubleton) and adopting upside-down count and attitude. I lead the ♠K, which asks partner to give count, and dummy is displayed:

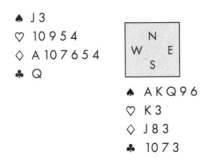

♠ J 3
♡ 10 9 5 4
♢ A 10 7 6 5 4
♣ Q

♠ A K Q 9 6
♡ K 3
♢ J 8 3
♣ 10 7 3

When I was a lad, no one would have contemplated bidding 3♢ with only six cards in the suit, not to mention a four-card major on the side, but try telling the youngsters of today that and they won't believe you.

Partner plays the ♠4 and declarer the two. I continue with the ♠Q and the trick is completed by the jack, ten and seven. If partner has the ♡A, the contract may well be down 'on the go', so I switch to the ♡K. Partner follows with the two and declarer wins with the ace and lays down the ♣A, followed by the king. When my partner follows with the ♣5 and ♣9, declarer proceeds to cash five more tricks in the suit. This is the position as the last one is played:

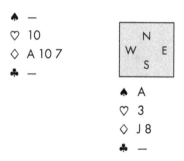

```
♠  —
♡  10
◇  A 10 7
♣  —
                    N
                W       E
                    S
♠  A
♡  3
◇  J 8
♣  —
```

A diamond is thrown from dummy and when my partner discards the ♡Q, declarer exits with the ♡7. North, down to ♡J ◇K9, has to win and return a diamond into the split tenace. This was the full deal:

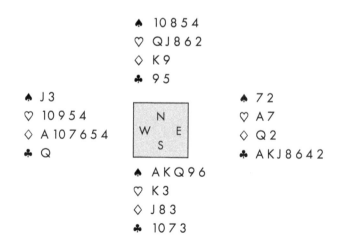

```
                ♠  10 8 5 4
                ♡  Q J 8 6 2
                ◇  K 9
                ♣  9 5
♠  J 3                           ♠  7 2
♡  10 9 5 4         N            ♡  A 7
◇  A 10 7 6 5 4  W     E         ◇  Q 2
♣  Q               S            ♣  A K J 8 6 4 2
                ♠  A K Q 9 6
                ♡  K 3
                ◇  J 8 3
                ♣  10 7 3
```

If partner had held the ♡A, three rounds of the suit would have resulted in two down — the best declarer can do is to ruff the third round high, cross to dummy with a club, cash the ◊A and then pitch a diamond on the ♡10. However, the sounder defense is for South to switch to the ♡3, which avoids the endplay. Switching to a diamond also works, but when declarer plays low from dummy and unblocks the queen under the king, North must return a diamond.

In the replay, West did not overcall but when North bid 3♠, East bid 4♣ anyway. Unfortunately, West thought this was non-leaping Michaels, promising clubs and hearts, and bid 4♡. This grisly contract finished four down, -200.

MODERN TIMES

At one time the English Bridge Union's Summer Festival included a friendly international match. During one such encounter I have unexpectedly been called into action for a set of boards. Fortunately, I know my partner's style, having watched her win more than one world title. We have avoided any major catastrophes so far when I pick up this hand as South:

Dealer West.
N-S Vul.

♠ K 10 5 4
♡ Q 9 4 2
◇ 10 5 2
♣ 4 2

When West opens 1♣, my partner doubles and East bids 1♠. Despite my modest values, I do have four hearts, and I elect to double to show them. In former times, this would have been a penalty double, promising at least four spades, but the modern approach is to treat it as a responsive double. When West rebids 2♣, my partner has nothing to say and East's raise to 3♣ sees West advance with 3◇. When East continues with 3♠, West's 3NT concludes the bidding:

West	North	East	South
1♣	dbl	1♠	dbl*
2♣	pass	3♣	pass
3◇	pass	3♠	pass
3NT	all pass		

My partner leads the ♠2 and dummy is revealed:

	♠ A Q 7 6 3
N	♡ 10 6 3
W E	◇ 3
S	♣ A 9 8 5

♠ K 10 5 4
♡ Q 9 4 2
◇ 10 5 2
♣ 4 2

When declarer puts in the queen, I win with the king, declarer following with the ♠8, and switch to a low diamond, which goes to the nine and queen. My partner returns the ♠J and that holds the trick, declarer discarding the ◇4. Declarer wins the next spade, pitching the ♡8, cashes the ♣A and plays a club back to the king, partner discarding the ◇6 on the second round. When the last of declarer's six clubs settles on the table, this is the position:

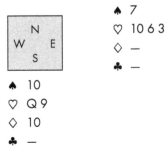

	♠ 7
	♡ 10 6 3
	◇ —
	♣ —

♠ 10
♡ Q 9
◇ 10
♣ —

My partner makes the spectacular discard of the ♡A, but declarer shows his cards, claiming nine tricks when this proves to be the original layout:

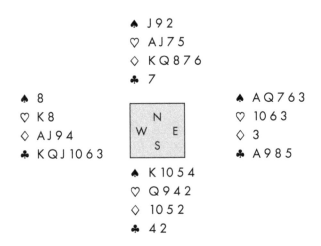

♠ J 9 2
♡ A J 7 5
◇ K Q 8 7 6
♣ 7

♠ 8
♡ K 8
◇ A J 9 4
♣ K Q J 10 6 3

♠ A Q 7 6 3
♡ 10 6 3
◇ 3
♣ A 9 8 5

♠ K 10 5 4
♡ Q 9 4 2
◇ 10 5 2
♣ 4 2

One of the debates in the modern era is North's choice of action over 1♣ on this type of hand. Assuming you want to enter the auction, do you overcall or double? On this occasion, the double had the advantage of getting all three suits into the picture.

When declarer cashed the last club, this was the situation:

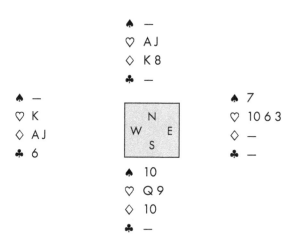

If North pitches the ♡J, declarer exits with the ♡K and scores the last two tricks.

Let's rewind to Trick 2. Whilst it is true that West's 3◇ might have been based on fewer than four cards, his subsequent bid of 3NT, promising a heart guard, suggested that there was some disparity in the length of his red suits. When you add that to North's initial double it seems clear that partner must have four hearts, which suggests that South might have found the killing switch to a low heart.

At the other table, they reached 5♣. On a trump lead, declarer can win in hand and crossruff diamonds and spades. North's ◇K start allowed declarer a minor variation, as he won and returned the ◇J, covered and ruffed. A trump to hand followed by another diamond ruff saw the appearance of South's ten, allowing declarer to claim.

65   FALSE IMPRESSION

My partner in a one-day teams event is a formidable player. He reminds me of the statement about his troops attributed to the Duke of Wellington before the battle of Waterloo: 'I don't know what effect they'll have on the enemy but, by God, they frighten me.' I am South, and in an early round I hold:

Dealer North.	♠ A 10 4 2
Neither Vul.	♡ A 9
	◇ Q 8 7 3
	♣ 10 8 2

When neither my partner nor East has anything to say, I briefly consider opening 1◇. However, experience has taught me that these 'third-hand' operations tend only to help the opposition, and when I pass, West opens 1♣. East responds 1◇ and, when West rebids 2NT promising 17-18, he rebids 3♡. After a brief pause, West advances to 3NT, giving us this sequence:

West	North	East	South
	pass	pass	pass
1♣	pass	1◇	pass
2NT	pass	3♡	pass
3NT	all pass		

My partner leads a fourth-best ♣4 and dummy is shapely, but short on points:

♠ Q J 6
♡ 8 6 3 2
◇ K J 10 6 5 4
♣ —

♠ A 10 4 2
♡ A 9
◇ Q 8 7 3
♣ 10 8 2

East had an awkward bid over 2NT. Apart from 3♡, he might also have chosen a pass or a scientific 3♠.

Declarer discards a heart from dummy and when I play the ♣10, he wins with the jack, cashes the ◇A and continues with the two. After following with the ◇9, partner discards the ♣3 and when declarer puts in dummy's jack, I win with the queen.

A player who leads around to declarer's first-bid suit usually has a strong holding, but partner's discard indicates that is not the case this time. Declarer has indicated 17-18 points, which leaves partner with 5 or 6. He should have an honor in clubs for his lead of the ♣4, so his remaining points will be in the majors. As to declarer's hand, I know he started with five clubs and two diamonds, leaving six cards in the majors. The 3NT bid suggests a stopper in the spade suit, which must be the ♠K. If declarer's clubs are headed by the ♣AKJ, then he may only have the ♡Q. Combining that with the possibility that the discard of the ♣3 is a suit-preference signal for hearts, I cash the ♡A and continue with the ♡9. Declarer wins with the king and plays a spade. Partner takes that with the king and returns the ♡J, but declarer wins with the queen and plays a second spade. I win with the ace, but declarer shows his cards, claiming the rest.

This was the layout:

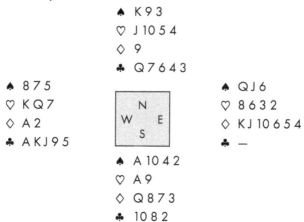

South's analysis was sound as far as it went, but further thought would have revealed that there was no rush to attempt to cash out. It is safe to switch to a spade at Trick 4. If partner cannot produce the king, South will still have time to take the ♠A and try for three (or four) tricks in hearts. It was the old story — when you have found a good move, look for a better one.

The bidding and play to the first three tricks were identical in the other room, but then South did switch to a spade. The defenders played three rounds of the suit, establishing the ♠10 as the setting trick when South came in with the ♡A.

Panic Stations

The major pairs events at the US Nationals attract exceptional fields. During the semifinal rounds of one of them, I pick up this South hand:

Dealer West.	♠ J 8 4
E-W Vul.	♡ 7 6
	◇ K 10 6
	♣ K Q 6 3 2

When West opens 1♡, East ponders for awhile before jumping to 4NT. When his partner responds 5♣, promising zero or three keycards, he continues with 5NT, asking about side kings. When West can only bid 6♡, East deliberates further before concluding matters with a jump to 7♠. This has been the spectacular auction:

West	North	East	South
1♡	pass	4NT*	pass
5♣*	pass	5NT*	pass
6♡*	pass	7♠	all pass

I eschew the traditional (but perhaps overrated) lead of a trump in favor of the ♣K, to reveal this dummy:

♠ 9 3
♡ A K 8 5 2
◇ Q J 9 8 4
♣ A

```
      N
  W       E
      S
```

♠ J 8 4
♡ 7 6
◇ K 10 6
♣ K Q 6 3 2

Declarer wins with dummy's ace perforce, playing the ♣4 from his hand as partner follows with the ♣9. After due consideration, declarer plays dummy's ◇Q, raising my hopes, but when partner follows with the ◇2 he plays the ◊A and ruffs the ♣5 in dummy, partner playing the seven. Declarer now cashes the ♡AK, pitching the ◊5, ruffs a diamond, ruffs the ♣J, ruffs a diamond and then presents the ♠A, claiming when we both follow.

This is how the cards were disposed originally:

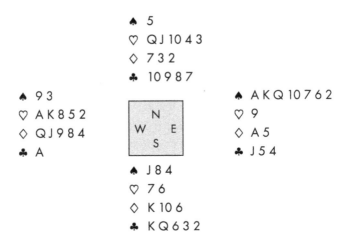

```
                    ♠ 5
                    ♡ QJ 10 4 3
                    ◊ 7 3 2
                    ♣ 10 9 8 7
  ♠ 9 3                            ♠ A K Q 10 7 6 2
  ♡ A K 8 5 2        N             ♡ 9
  ◊ Q J 9 8 4    W       E         ◊ A 5
  ♣ A                S             ♣ J 5 4
                    ♠ J 8 4
                    ♡ 7 6
                    ◊ K 10 6
                    ♣ K Q 6 3 2
```

POST-MORTEM

A trump lead against a grand slam may be overrated, but here it would have ensured declarer's downfall.

Several pairs bid the grand slam and those who did not receive a trump lead made the contract, save for the declarer who saw the ◊K appear when he ruffed the ◊Q! He cashed the ♠A and ruffed his final club. Now he decided that the safest way to return to hand to draw trumps was to ruff the third round of hearts but was disabused when South over-ruffed.

That was a brilliant recovery by South, but if declarer had given full weight to North's play on the first round of diamonds it might not have succeeded.

Playing in a long Swiss Teams event in Madeira, a series of winning scorecards from our teammates have seen us advance to the top of the leaderboard. My partner is keen, but sometimes lacks confidence. My first set of cards sitting South is nothing special:

Dealer West.	♠ J 7 6
Neither Vul.	♡ J 6
	◇ A 9 8 5 4
	♣ Q 9 3

When West opens 1♡, East replies with a game-forcing 2◇ and then bids a fourth-suit 3♠ over West's 3♣ rebid. That sees the opener advance to 3NT. The simple auction was:

West	North	East	South
1♡	pass	2◇ *	pass
3♣	pass	3♠ *	pass
3NT	all pass		

My partner leads a fourth-best ♠2 to reveal this dummy:

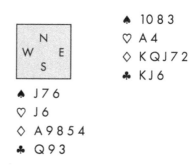

```
              ♠ 10 8 3
              ♡ A 4
      N       ◇ K Q J 7 2
    W   E     ♣ K J 6
      S
  ♠ J 7 6
  ♡ J 6
  ◇ A 9 8 5 4
  ♣ Q 9 3
```

Declarer plays low from dummy, takes my jack with the queen and plays the ◇3 to the six, king and my ace. I return the ♠7 and, when declarer follows with the nine, my partner produces the king and then switches to the ♣4. When declarer plays low from dummy, I put in the queen and am pleased to see it hold. I return my last spade and declarer wins with the ace, crosses to dummy with the ♡A, cashes the top diamonds and then plays a heart, claiming when my jack appears.

This was the full deal:

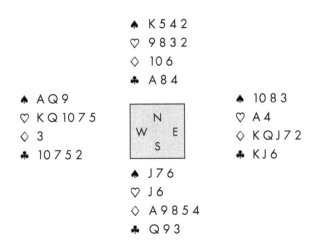

```
                    ♠ K 5 4 2
                    ♡ 9 8 3 2
                    ◇ 10 6
                    ♣ A 8 4
    ♠ A Q 9                          ♠ 10 8 3
    ♡ K Q 10 7 5         N          ♡ A 4
    ◇ 3            W         E       ◇ K Q J 7 2
    ♣ 10 7 5 2          S           ♣ K J 6
                    ♠ J 7 6
                    ♡ J 6
                    ◇ A 9 8 5 4
                    ♣ Q 9 3
```

POST-MORTEM

There is no legitimate way to defeat the contract, but nevertheless, at the other table the defenders found a way to deflect declarer from the right path. The defense followed an identical course up to the point where declarer crossed to the ♡A, but this time South followed with the ♡J! Convinced that he could no longer hope for five heart tricks, declarer needed to score a trick in clubs. As North had failed to clear the spade suit, it seemed logical to place the ace with South, so declarer played the ♣K. However, it was North who took the trick and his last spade defeated the 'unbeatable' game.

As to declarer's play, one could argue that when North switched to a club it was better to go up with dummy's ♣K, as in this situation it is much more likely that he is leading away from the ace than the queen.

CONFIDENCE TRICK

68

The European Open Championships are always keenly contested, and afford one an opportunity to travel to fascinating cities across the continent. During the qualifying rounds of the teams event, I pick up this shapely collection in the South chair:

Dealer West.	♠ A J 8 5 4 3
Neither Vul.	♡ K 8 7 5 4
	♢ J 3
	♣ —

After two passes, East opens 1♣ and I have to consider the best way to describe my hand. I could overcall 1♠ and hope to introduce the hearts on the next round, but with a hand that is short on high cards I prefer to get both suits into the picture immediately and bid 2♣, which promises at least 5-5 in the majors. When West has nothing to say, my partner bids 3♠ and East doubles. I don't expect partner to have much in the way of high cards (he would start with 3♣ if he did) but he will have good spade support. I may not make it, but I decide to bid 4♠ anyway, and West now comes to life with 5♣, which ends proceedings:

West	North	East	South
pass	pass	1♣	2♣ *
pass	3♠	dbl	4♠
5♣	all pass		

I could lead the ♠A to look at dummy, but I consider leading an unsupported ace to be usually unsound, even when my suit has been raised. Leading away from a king is unthinkable, so I decide to start with the ♢J:

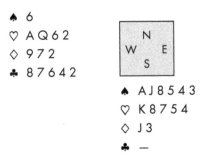

    ♠ 6
    ♡ A Q 6 2
    ◊ 9 7 2
    ♣ 8 7 6 4 2

    ♠ A J 8 5 4 3
    ♡ K 8 7 5 4
    ◊ J 3
    ♣ —

The first trick is completed by the two, eight and five. When I continue with the ◊3, declarer takes partner's queen with the ace and plays the ♡10. I play low in tempo, and when declarer calls for dummy's two, I await partner's card with interest. It proves to be the ♡9 and declarer now proceeds to draw trumps in three rounds, partner playing the three, nine and jack. When he produces the ♡J, I cover with the king, but declarer wins with dummy's ace, pitches a spade on the ♡Q and ruffs a heart. These cards remain:

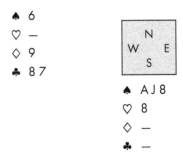

    ♠ 6
    ♡ —
    ◊ 9
    ♣ 8 7

    ♠ A J 8
    ♡ 8
    ◊ —
    ♣ —

Declarer now produces the ♠K. I can win, but must then offer up a ruff and discard. This was the full deal:

```
                 ♠ Q 9 7 2
                 ♡ 9 3
                 ◇ K Q 8 6
                 ♣ J 9 3
   ♠ 6                              ♠ K 10
   ♡ A Q 6 2        ┌─────────┐      ♡ J 10
   ◇ 9 7 2          │    N    │      ◇ A 10 5 4
   ♣ 8 7 6 4 2      │ W     E │      ♣ A K Q 10 5
                    │    S    │
                    └─────────┘
                 ♠ A J 8 5 4 3
                 ♡ K 8 7 5 4
                 ◇ J 3
                 ♣ —
```

POST-MORTEM

If South covers the ♡10, declarer can win with dummy's ace, but with no quick trump entry to dummy it is impossible to reach the same ending, and the loss of three tricks becomes unavoidable.

As I suspected, leading the ♠A would not have been a triumph, but annoyingly an initial heart lead does no damage, as long as the defenders are careful.

A 4♠ contract by North should go down. On the lead of a top club, declarer can ruff and play a diamond to the queen, but East wins and switches to the ♡J, subsequently overruffing dummy on the third round of the suit.

69

DÉJÀ VU

The biennial Monaco Cavendish Pairs is one of the richest events in the bridge calendar, offering the potential of huge cash prizes to those who are willing to pay the sizeable entry fee. As the Principality contains some of my favorite restaurants, I have persuaded a strong client to foot the bill. With a following wind, we have qualified for the final, where finishing in the top seven will more than cover our expenses. We are in sight of our goal when I pick up these cards as South:

Dealer East.
N-S Vul.

♠ J 10 5 3
♡ 9 5
◊ K 6 4 3
♣ K 10 6

East opens 1♣ and, when West responds 1♡, East jumps to 3◊, promising four-card heart support and diamond shortage. West cuebids 3♠ and East continues with 4◊, indicating that he has a first-round control. In this situation, John Armstrong suggested that a double should ask partner to lead the suit below the splinter. Although I have discussed this with my current partner, I am not sure we have agreed to add it to our relatively small list of agreements. I decide to venture a double, as in any event a diamond lead is unlikely to give anything away. West continues with a keycard ask of 4NT and, when East admits to three of them with 5◊, he advances to 6♡, leaving us with this auction:

West	North	East	South
		1♣	pass
1♡	pass	3◊*	pass
3♠*	pass	4◊*	dbl
4NT*	pass	5◊*	pass
6♡	all pass		

My partner leads the ♡3:

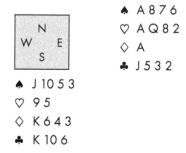

♠ A 8 7 6
♡ A Q 8 2
◊ A
♣ J 5 3 2

♠ J 10 5 3
♡ 9 5
◊ K 6 4 3
♣ K 10 6

It seems my double has not registered as anything significant and a trump lead is generally a sound stratagem against a 4-4-4-1 pattern.

Declarer wins with dummy's ace and calls for the ♣2, putting in the eight when I follow with the six. Partner wins with the queen and exits with the ♡7. Declarer wins in hand with the jack, crosses to the ◊A, plays a spade to the king, ruffs a diamond, returns to hand with the ♠Q, ruffs a diamond, crosses back with the ♣A and draws the outstanding trump with the ♡K. These cards remain:

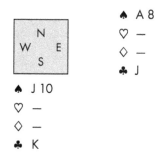

♠ A 8
♡ —
◊ —
♣ J

♠ J 10
♡ —
◊ —
♣ K

Declarer now plays the ♡6, discarding dummy's ♣J. I try throwing the ♣K, but declarer shows his cards, claiming the last two tricks with the ♣9 and dummy's ♠A.

The full deal:

```
                    ♠ 9 2
                    ♡ 10 7 3
                    ◇ 9 8 7 5 2
                    ♣ Q 7 4
      ♠ K Q 4                         ♠ A 8 7 6
      ♡ K J 6 4        ┌─────────┐    ♡ A Q 8 2
      ◇ Q J 10         │    N    │    ◇ A
      ♣ A 9 8          │ W     E │    ♣ J 5 3 2
                       │    S    │
                       └─────────┘
                    ♠ J 10 5 3
                    ♡ 9 5
                    ◇ K 6 4 3
                    ♣ K 10 6
```

POST-MORTEM

Partner recalled our discussion, but was not confident we had an agreement. A pity, as the lead of a low club would have been too much for declarer. However, I could also have sunk the ship by inserting the ♣10 at Trick 2! If declarer ducks, I can continue with just about anything (except the ◇K!).

Safety Last

70

Playing in an online event, my partner is a solid, if somewhat unimaginative player; our opponents do not normally offer up too many opportunities. My collection sitting South is distinctly average:

Dealer South.	♠	8 5 2
N-S Vul.	♡	K 10 6 4
	◇	Q J 6
	♣	A 10 7

With these cards, I can only pass and hope to be on the winning side. West and my partner make no contribution, but East opens 2♠, which turns out to be a prehistoric Acol two-bid, promising eight playing tricks. West raises to 3♠ and East rebids 4♣, promising a control in the suit. I decide to double that and, when West cuebids 4◇, East replies with 4♡ and West bids 4♠. After brief reflection, East advances to 6♠, leaving us with this auction:

West	North	East	South
			pass
pass	pass	2♠ *	pass
3♠	pass	4♣ *	dbl
4◇ *	pass	4♡ *	pass
4♠	pass	6♠	all pass

As I have the ♣A, declarer's 4♣ must be based on a void, singleton or the ♣K. With defensive cards in all three side suits and most of our side's combined assets, I lead a trump:

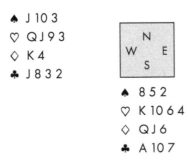

```
    ♠ J 10 3
    ♡ Q J 9 3              N
    ◇ K 4            W         E
    ♣ J 8 3 2              S
                     ♠ 8 5 2
                     ♡ K 10 6 4
                     ◇ Q J 6
                     ♣ A 10 7
```

Declarer plays dummy's ♠3. When partner follows with the ♠6, declarer wins with the seven, plays a diamond to the king, a diamond to the ace and then ruffs the ◇10, partner following with the five, two and three. Declarer now proceeds to play spades, partner parting with five cards, the ♡5, ♡7, ◇8, ♣4 and ♣5. These cards remain:

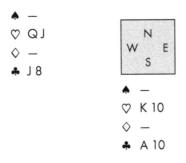

```
    ♠ —
    ♡ Q J                  N
    ◇ —              W         E
    ♣ J 8                  S
                     ♠ —
                     ♡ K 10
                     ◇ —
                     ♣ A 10
```

Declarer now produces the ◇9. If I throw the ♡10, declarer can discard a club and cash the ♡A I know he must have. Parting with the ♣10 will allow declarer to exit with a club and I will have to lead away from the ♡K. In desperation, I discard the ♣A, but declarer now shows his cards, claiming the two tricks he needs with the ♡A and the ♣K.

This was the full deal:

```
                    ♠ 6
                    ♡ 8 7 5
                    ◇ 8 5 3 2
                    ♣ Q 9 6 5 4
  ♠ J 10 3                          ♠ A K Q 9 7 4
  ♡ Q J 9 3          N              ♡ A 2
  ◇ K 4          W       E          ◇ A 10 9 7
  ♣ J 8 3 2          S              ♣ K
                    ♠ 8 5 2
                    ♡ K 10 6 4
                    ◇ Q J 6
                    ♣ A 10 7
```

POST-MORTEM

Given that he would be on lead against a spade contract, South's double was unnecessary. It gave declarer an important clue, which combined with the passive trump lead was enough to point towards the winning line.

As is so often the case, the opening lead was decisive — if South had selected the ♣A, declarer would have had to rely on the losing heart finesse.

The Young Chelsea Bridge Club has long been recognized as one of the best in London, and its Friday night IMP Pairs is when the stars come out to play. My partner is a fine player, who happens to own a vineyard in France. The player on my right has more than one world title to her name. My hand sitting South is nothing special:

Dealer North.	♠ Q 4
E-W Vul.	♡ K 10 8 7 6
	◇ A Q 9 8
	♣ 9 5

After my partner passes, East opens 1♣ and I overcall 1♡. When West bids 3NT, East continues with 4♣, and when West cuebids 4♡ she jumps to 6♣, giving us this sequence:

West	North	East	South
		1♣	1♡
3NT	pass	4♣	pass
4♡*	pass	6♣	all pass

Leading a spade might work if partner has the king, but otherwise is likely to help declarer, and a trump is too passive for my liking. The ◇A is a possibility, but if declarer has a doubleton king it could be catastrophic. Although my dislike for leading away from a king is well chronicled, here it appears to be the least of evils and I start with the ♡7:

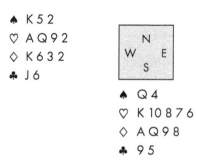

♠ K 5 2
♡ A Q 9 2
◇ K 6 3 2
♣ J 6

♠ Q 4
♡ K 10 8 7 6
◇ A Q 9 8
♣ 9 5

Declarer calls for dummy's queen and partner follows with the jack. After drawing trumps in three rounds, declarer plays a spade to the king and a spade to the jack, partner following with the six and three. I win with the queen and cash the ◇A — at least I attempt to, but declarer ruffs, cashes two more clubs, crosses to dummy with the ♡A, pitches a heart on the ◇K and then plays a spade to the nine, claiming the last trick with the ♠A.

The full deal:

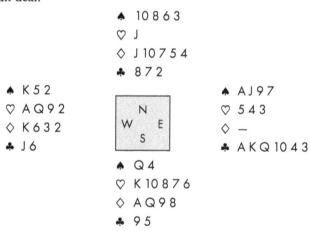

♠ 10 8 6 3
♡ J
◇ J 10 7 5 4
♣ 8 7 2

♠ K 5 2
♡ A Q 9 2
◇ K 6 3 2
♣ J 6

♠ A J 9 7
♡ 5 4 3
◇ —
♣ A K Q 10 4 3

♠ Q 4
♡ K 10 8 7 6
◇ A Q 9 8
♣ 9 5

There are several reasons why attempting to cash the ◇A was wrong. The fact that declarer made no attempt to ask for keycards strongly suggested she held a void. More to the point, assuming partner's ♡J was a singleton, the play in spades showed that North held four cards in the suit and therefore declarer could be counted for a 4=3=0=6 shape. What South has to do is return the ♡K, severing declarer's link to the dummy.

Declarer, too, could have done better. After drawing trumps she should cash the ♠A, play a spade to the king and then play a spade. If North has the queen he can win, but has no heart to play. On a diamond return, declarer ruffs and plays her winners in the black suits to reach this position:

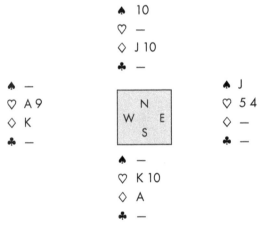

When she plays the ♠J, South has no answer.

NOT PAST THE IRON DUKE 72

Playing in trials for the European Teams Championships I pick up a decent hand as South:

Dealer East.	♠ A 9 8 7 3
Neither Vul.	♡ A Q
	◇ 8 3 2
	♣ A 9 5

When East opens 1◇, I overcall 1♠. West has nothing to say, but my partner jumps to 4♡. East comes again with 5◇ and I have to choose between a mildly conservative pass, an aggressive 5♡ or a speculative double. Partner's bid is preemptive in nature, showing no ambition, so I don't immediately see where an eleventh trick might come from, although it might be possible to establish a long spade. With three aces I decide to double, which ends proceedings:

West	North	East	South
		1◇	1♠
pass	4♡	5◇	dbl
all pass			

I lead the ♡A and dummy is revealed:

♠ K Q J 10 6
♡ 8 7 5
◇ 7
♣ Q 10 6 3

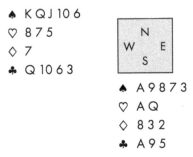

♠ A 9 8 7 3
♡ A Q
◇ 8 3 2
♣ A 9 5

Declarer ruffs and plays the ♣7. When I follow with the five, he plays dummy's ten and partner can only produce the four. A diamond to the queen is followed by the ◇A and, when partner's second card in the suit turns out to be the king, declarer shows his cards, acknowledging that we will score two aces.

This was the full deal:

♠ 2
♡ K J 10 9 6 4 3 2
◇ K 4
♣ 4 2

♠ K Q J 10 6
♡ 8 7 5
◇ 7
♣ Q 10 6 3

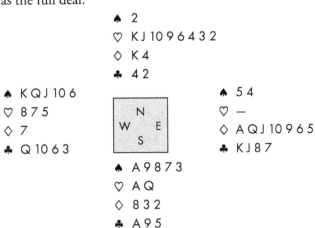

♠ 5 4
♡ —
◇ A Q J 10 9 6 5
♣ K J 8 7

♠ A 9 8 7 3
♡ A Q
◇ 8 3 2
♣ A 9 5

South needed to rise with the ♣A and switch to ace and another spade, enabling North to ruff. I should have spotted that, but partner could have helped by playing the ♡K under the ace.

In the other room, South decided to bid on to 5♡. That is easily defeated if East starts with two rounds of diamonds, but instead he opted to lead the ♠5. Declarer won with dummy's ace and ruffed a spade high. He went back to dummy with the ♡A and ruffed another spade before running the trumps. This was the four-card ending:

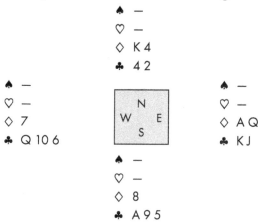

When declarer played the ♣2, East fatally followed with the jack and, after winning with dummy's ace, declarer played a second club. East won but had to surrender the game-going trick in diamonds.

Playing in an event in Cairo, my vivacious partner is making a name for herself. At one point we encounter an opponent not unconnected with the film industry and are surrounded by spectators. The women are watching the actor, while the men only have eyes for my partner. My collection in the South seat is nothing to write home about:

Dealer South.	♠ 7 5 4 3 2
N-S Vul.	♡ 9 6
	◇ 9 8 2
	♣ A 9 8

West opens 1♠ and my partner overcalls 2♡. East has nothing to say, but when I pass, West reopens with a double. I am relieved to see East bid 2NT, which is alerted and explained as Lebensohl — a request for West to bid 3♣, after which East will clarify her hand. West goes past 3♣ by bidding 3◇, which promises a strong hand. East raises to 4◇, suggesting a modest hand with good trump support, and that is enough for West to go on to 5◇:

West	North	East	South
			pass
1♠	2♡	pass	pass
dbl	pass	2NT*	pass
3◇*	pass	4◇	pass
5◇	all pass		

My partner leads the ♣Q and dummy is much as expected:

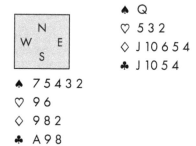

```
            ♠ Q
            ♡ 5 3 2
            ◇ J 10 6 5 4
            ♣ J 10 5 4
    ♠ 7 5 4 3 2
    ♡ 9 6
    ◇ 9 8 2
    ♣ A 9 8
```

In our methods, the ♣Q indicates possession of the ♣K and asks for attitude (the ♣K would request a count signal). When I encourage with the ♣9, partner continues with the ♣7, but declarer ruffs my ♣A and cashes the ◇AK, partner following with the ◇3 and then discarding the ♡7. A spade to dummy's queen holds and declarer returns to hand with a diamond and cashes the ♠A. Partner played the nine on the first round of spades and when she produces the ♠10 on the next spade, declarer shows his cards:

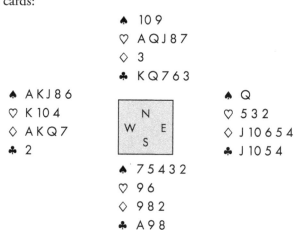

```
                ♠ 10 9
                ♡ A Q J 8 7
                ◇ 3
                ♣ K Q 7 6 3
♠ A K J 8 6                         ♠ Q
♡ K 10 4                            ♡ 5 3 2
◇ A K Q 7                           ◇ J 10 6 5 4
♣ 2                                 ♣ J 10 5 4
                ♠ 7 5 4 3 2
                ♡ 9 6
                ◇ 9 8 2
                ♣ A 9 8
```

To defeat 5◇, South must overtake the ♣Q and switch to a heart. Not a difficult play to find, but one of a type that is all too easily missed. It was suggested that North might have overcalled 2♠, promising at least 5-5 in hearts and a minor. That is a possibility, but North is opposite a passed hand, and the vulnerability is against it.

What do you make of declarer's line of play? If North had held say ♠92, declarer's line would have failed. After cashing one trump, declarer can cross to the ♠Q, ruff a club and then play the winning spades, discarding dummy's hearts. With diamonds 3-1 this leads to twelve tricks as declarer will be able to ruff another club, but even if North can ruff the second spade declarer will be safe for eleven tricks.

In the replay, East bid 3◇ over West's double and South's heart lead against 5◇ saw the defenders take the first four tricks.

The House of Peers

It is always an honor to be invited to the Houses of Parliament for the annual match between the Lords and Commons. Since I am still awaiting ennoblement, my role is necessarily confined to that of reporter. Having partaken of a splendid afternoon tea, I have resumed my seat behind an MP when he picks up these cards as South:

Dealer North.
E-W Vul.

♠ K 5 4 3
♡ K 10 4 3
◇ 6 4 3
♣ 7 3

Partner opens 1◇ and East overcalls 4♣. When West raises to 5♣, North doubles. With good support for both majors I am expecting South to bid 5♡ (following Edgar Kaplan's dictum, 'Takeout doubles should be taken out') but perhaps mindful of an old Bols Bridge Tip, 'The five-level belongs to the opponents', South elects to defend:

West	North	East	South
	1◇	4♣	pass
5♣	dbl	all pass	

With defensive cards in both majors, I would be tempted to lead a trump, hoping to cut down possible ruffs, but South prefers the ◇4 and this threatening dummy appears:

♠ Q 8 6
♡ Q J 9 8 7 6
◇ A
♣ K 5 2

```
        N
    W       E
        S
```

♠ K 5 4 3
♡ K 10 4 3
◇ 6 4 3
♣ 7 3

Winning perforce with dummy's ace, declarer plays the ♠6 to his jack, North following with the two. South wins with the king and belatedly switches to a trump, but declarer wins in hand as partner discards a diamond. He now proceeds to crossruff diamonds and spades before drawing the outstanding trump and claiming eleven tricks.

This was the full deal:

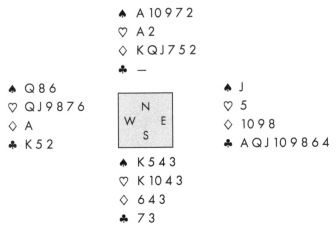

```
                    ♠ A 10 9 7 2
                    ♡ A 2
                    ◇ K Q J 7 5 2
                    ♣ —
 ♠ Q 8 6                               ♠ J
 ♡ Q J 9 8 7 6          N              ♡ 5
 ◇ A                W       E          ◇ 10 9 8
 ♣ K 5 2                S              ♣ A Q J 10 9 8 6 4
                    ♠ K 5 4 3
                    ♡ K 10 4 3
                    ◇ 6 4 3
                    ♣ 7 3
```

POST-MORTEM

My idea of leading a trump would have worked, provided North rises with the ace if declarer plays the ♡Q from dummy. He must then switch to a low spade so South can win and play a second trump. By contrast, North must play low if declarer tries a spade at Trick 2, so South can get in to play a second trump.

At another table, West did not raise 4♣ to 5♣, and North bid 4♠. Naturally, West now bid 5♣, but when South raised to 5♠, North decided to bid 'one more for the road' and went on to slam. South ruffed the club lead in dummy, played a spade to the king and finessed on the second round of trumps for a tremendous swing.

If it transpires that bridge becomes a game that is primarily played on the Internet, rest assured that the quality of play will remain extremely high. Playing with a student in one of the many online games that have proliferated during the COVID-19 outbreak, I see that I have a hand with potential as South:

Dealer East.	♠ A J 8 6 4
Neither Vul.	♡ A 5
	◇ Q 10 8 7 5
	♣ 7

However, East opens 3♠ and West's 3NT brings the auction to an end:

West	North	East	South
		3♠	pass
3NT	all pass		

When my partner leads a fourth-best ♡2, the sight of dummy makes it clear that declarer will have to do all the work himself:

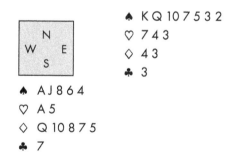

```
                        ♠ K Q 10 7 5 3 2
          ┌─────────┐   ♡ 7 4 3
          │   N     │   ◇ 4 3
          │ W     E │   ♣ 3
          │   S     │
          └─────────┘
          ♠ A J 8 6 4
          ♡ A 5
          ◇ Q 10 8 7 5
          ♣ 7
```

I win with the ♡A and declarer follows with the ♡8. This is one of those deals where it is possible to draw a number of inferences. The first is that declarer almost certainly has a long club suit. Secondly, it is unlikely that partner has a five-card suit — with five diamonds or clubs there would be no reason not to lead one (although one might prefer to lead a heart from, say, ♡KQ102 rather than a club from ♣86542). Thirdly, declarer obviously has at most one spade. If partner has the missing ♠9, then his shape is virtually guaranteed to be 1=4=4=4. To test my theory, I cash the ♠A and declarer discards the ♣4. In one way that's a pity, since if partner had been void it would have been possible for him to make a suit-preference signal. Although I think it is unlikely that my partner would lead the ♡2 from ♡KQJ2, it is certainly not impossible. (I once saw a World Champion lead the ♡2 from ♡AKQ2 against 3NT — when declarer played low from dummy's ♡J874, East won with the ten and returned a heart to put the contract down.) So, should I switch to a diamond or play back the ♡5?

Assuming partner is 1=4=4=4, then declarer must be 0=4=2=7. On that basis it must now be safe to switch to a diamond and that proves to be the winning defense.

The full deal:

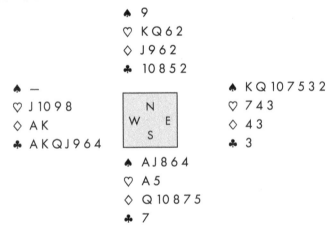

```
              ♠ 9
              ♡ K Q 6 2
              ◇ J 9 6 2
              ♣ 10 8 5 2
♠ —                              ♠ K Q 10 7 5 3 2
♡ J 10 9 8          N            ♡ 7 4 3
◇ A K           W       E        ◇ 4 3
♣ A K Q J 9 6 4     S            ♣ 3
              ♠ A J 8 6 4
              ♡ A 5
              ◇ Q 10 8 7 5
              ♣ 7
```

POST-MORTEM

Cashing the ♠A at Trick 2 resulted in declarer being squeezed, and his nine tricks suddenly became eight! Having suffered through the previous seventy-four deals, Ron Tacchi, my archetypal Joe Public, emerged triumphant on the final problem.

So, I hope, did you.